M000082452

Praise

for **Serene Makeover: Inner Edition** **Feng Shui Your Life From the Inside Out**

"Ariel Joseph Towne is the Wayne Dyer of our generation. He has a way of taking ancient spiritual principles and practices and making them both tangible and transformative for modern life. In this book, he makes a passionate case that we can have it all. Within the first few pages, I already felt moved to believe that for myself! *Serene Makeover: Inner Edition* is a practical blueprint for manifesting the life you have always wanted."

—Julie Zipper
Licensed Agape practitioner, juliezipper.com
Author of **Astro Zen** and co-founder of Earth School

....

"I have had the pleasure of being one of Ariel's clients, as well as co-creating a Shui-Meets-Yoga course with him. I can say from both sides of the coin that he is easily one of the most authentic, life-changing people I know; one whose improvement-wisdom extends the full spectrum from home to relationships, wealth, personal and career success and more. I highly recommend this book for anyone who wants to turbo-boost their lives to the next, most prosperous level, starting today."

—Sadie Nardini
yoga and ultimate wellness expert, sadienardini.com
Host of "Rock Your Yoga" on Veria TV

....

Serene Makeover: Inner Edition, Feng Shui Your Life From the Inside Out helped bring me so much comfort and balance during my difficult divorce. Whether you are going through a tough time and need some wisdom and support or just looking for some internal tuning, you will finish this book feeling energized. Ariel Joseph Towne helped me tap into my power from within. Thank you."

—Jessica Denay
Author of the **Hot Mom's Handbook** series

"If I could, I would make this a must-read for all of my students. It's truly inspiring. Even reading it makes one feel calmer."

—Warner Loughlin
Celebrity Acting Coach, CEO Warner Loughlin Studios

"Our health and wellness are not only dictated by the flow of electrical signals within the body, but also the energy system of our environment. In *Serene Makeover: Inner Edition, Feng Shui Your Life From the Inside Out*, Ariel empowers us to change our outer world in order to transform our inner world. With his expert guidance, learn how easy it can be to remove what is blocking the flow of your life."

—Randall Zamcheck
CEO, Body Ecology, LLC

"Ariel has keen insight when it comes to cultivating balance and happiness in human beings. His strong innate intuition blends with down to earth wisdom, offering his readers sound and helpful tools for navigating with finesse the inner and outer life situations of this human experience."

—Olivia Rosewood
Meditation expert, huffingtonpost.com/olivia-rosewood
Author of **Please Meditate: It's Good for You** and **Happy Yoga:
7 Reasons Why There's Nothing to Worry About** (with Steve Ross)

"Ariel has taught me so much about balance. Balance in my home, my office and my own skin. After doing sessions with him, I met the love of my life and my company took a turn for greater success. I am so pleased he is sharing his guidance with everyone who is not as lucky as I am to have him on speed dial. As he mentions in his book, we define our own limitations. I am sure that the positive impact he will have with his first book is truly limitless."

—Sophie Chiche
Founder and curator, lifebyme.com

....

"It's virtually impossible to follow Ariel's wisdom and NOT have your life transformed for the better. Read this and start today!"

—Michelle Fiordaliso, MSW
Licensed psychotherapist, michellefiordaliso.com
Co-author of **Everything You Always Wanted to Know About Ex**
and 2008 recipient of a PEN USA award for fiction.

....

serene
makeover: INNER EDITION

feng shui your life from the inside out

ARIEL JOSEPH TOWNE

Copyright 2012 by Ariel Joseph Towne

All rights reserved
Printed in the United States of America
First Edition

For information about permission to reproduce sections
from this book or for special discounts for bulk purchases, write to:

THE FENG SHUI GUY
Ariel Joseph Towne
9903 Santa Monica Blvd. #638
Beverly Hills, CA, 90212

ISBN-13: 978-0985808846

Self published by Ariel Joseph Towne—The Feng Shui Guy

For more information about The Feng Shui Guy: Ariel Joseph Towne or to book a consultation, please visit: thefengshuiguy.com

COMING SOON:

Feng Shui for Health (audio CD/download)
Feng Shui for Business (audio CD/download)
Feng Shui for Love (audio CD/download)
Personal Revolution: 21 Days to Transform Your Life Inside and Out (DVD)

BOOKS ARIEL HAS CONTRIBUTED TO:

ORGANIZING *One Year to an Organized Life With Baby* by Regina Leeds
SELF DISCOVERY *Road Trip Guide to the Soul* by Sadie Nardini
PARENTING *The Hot Moms-to-Be Handbook:*
Look and Feel Great From Bump to Baby by Jessica Denay
SENSUALITY AND SEX *Sex Beyond the Missionary* by Eva Christina

Dedications

To **Miles Meilinger**, whose inner light shines so brightly.

I've known Miles since I was 1 ½-years-old. He is an incredible storyteller, musician, artisan, businessman, father, husband and friend. It's because of his love for his wife Judy (and vice versa) that I came to believe that having a life-long relationship was possible for me. Miles is someone who has been able to make a living his whole life by doing what he loves to do. When Miles is hugging me, the worries of the world suddenly disappear. He is part of my extended family and I am grateful for his humor, his wisdom and his presence.

Miles is someone who rarely complains, who seems to find the good in any circumstance and has never seemed to let life's challenges dampen his spirit. He lives the expression: "your outer reality doesn't have to dictate your inner experience." Miles has been showing up recently in several of my meditations. Even though we live on opposite sides of the country, I know that distance will never affect our closeness. Miles, thank you for being you.

Also **Erin Cardillo Towne**, who reminds me that I am redonkulously magical. I am inspired by who my wife is in the world. She is an incredibly gifted actress, writer and teacher. She is playful and creative and good hearted. She cares about people and wants their happiness, success and well-being. She believes in magic and possibility and I love sharing my dreams and big ideas with her.

Every part of my life has gotten better since she and I started dating. She was the inspiration for the philosophy behind this book. It was falling in love with her mind, her spirit and her beauty that made me imagine that having a life that is fulfilling on all levels was possible.

1

Appreciation

Thank you, **Crystal Star Towne** (mom, spiritual advisor and jedi teacher.). I feel you around me as I meditate on and write these pages. Thank you for the many adventures we had in our short time together. Thank you for always teaching me by example. I am still unfolding the deep wisdom contained within our many conversations. I love you always and forever and a day.

Thank you, **Sanford Fagin** (my dad). Your brush with near death showed me what is possible when it comes to inner transformation. Your willpower and determination to stay on the planet borders on the miraculous. Love you, daddio.

Thank you, **Joe Towne** (also my dad). For as long as I can remember, you have always been an excellent example of balance. I thank you for showing me the importance of speaking up and communicating instead of holding things inside. Love you so, poppa Joe.

Thank you, **William D. Littleford**. You ingrained in me the importance of education, the concept of "grandma manners" and the reminder to always be mindful of the needs of other people.

Thank you, **Master Nate Batoon and the Feng Shui Family,** for introducing me to the world of feng shui and helping me to believe in myself. Thank you to Nate in particular for being my personal Yoda. May the force be with you, always.

Thank you, **Yasuhiko Kimura**, for helping me tap the secrets of the universe, for helping me listen to the passion that lies within my heart and for challenging me to a life of authentic creativity.

Thank you, **Warner Loughlin**, for helping me remember myself when I was filled with doubt and fear. Thank you for holding space for my light to emerge. Thank you for introducing me to my wife.

Thank you, **Thomas Ashley Farrand**, for being such a profound teacher of the power of words and mantras. Thank you for your blessings, your wisdom and the induction into the art of Sanksrit mantra.

Thank you, **Professor Lin Yun**, for helping bring feng shui to the west so that I could learn from you. I am so grateful for your teachings, both in person and through others. Om Mani Padme Hum.

Thank you, **Cheryl King**, for being my most significant writing teacher. Through our many conversations, I have become a much better person and a man in the world. Love you, momma K.

Thank you, **Regina Leeds**, for encouraging me all these many years to write a book. I adore you!

Thank you beyond measure, **Maureen Healy, editor extraordinaire**. I simply could not have written this book without you. You were such an incredible part of this book throughout its conception, development and execution. You were one of the first people I spoke to about this concept. Your willingness to create its structure, transcribe tens of hours worth of conversations and to toil over each word to ensure its clarity has been the most incredible gift to me. I am so incredibly grateful for your wisdom and mad skills as editor.

Thank you, **Lisa Knight, designer and graphic artist**, for your incredible talents, your passion for working on this project and for your painstaking detail to its design and beauty.

Thank you, **Rod Menzies, my teacher**, for helping me embrace my shadow and for your encouragement in having conversations in my life that I never thought were possible before.

Thank you, **Laura Smith**, for giving me an opportunity to be on the radio and for being the first person to ever tell me I should write a book about feng shui.

Thank you, **Philip Isles**, for the birthday adventure that started this journey of writing this book. I'll never forget it as long as I live.

Thank you, **Arnie and Deb Cardillo**, for everything you have done behind the scenes, including offering your insights, wisdom and encouragement throughout the design, naming and proofreading of this book.

Thank you, **Eric Myers**, for believing so strongly in the concept of feng shui for your inner house.

Thank you, **Gina Sorrel**, for your incredible friendship and support through the years, including (but not limited to) your help in clarifying the name of this book.

Thank you, **Jessica Denay**, for your help in branding myself The Feng Shui Guy. I cherished our many conversations until the wee hours. Thanks for your encouragement, loving kindness and all your help in sharing my work with the world.

Thank you, **Sadie Nardini**, for being my yogi rockstar and for your ongoing wisdom and partnership through so many workshops, adventures and collaborations. I cherish our connection and am so grateful for your presence in my life.

Thank you, **Randall Zamcheck**, for your wisdom, your friendship and your encouragement. I appreciate your dedication to the health and well-being of those you care for. Namaste, dude.

Thank you, **Julie Zipper**, for your deep friendship, vast wisdom and your great big heart. I appreciate your consistent reaffirmation that the universe is always working for our good.

Thank you, **Terry Towne**, for being so encouraging of my dreams through the years. I would not have been able to consult, teach and develop these insights without your loving support.

Thank you to **all of my clients, friends and colleagues** for the opportunity to learn from you; for the opportunity to express these principles which were offered to me; and for allowing me to witness your heartache, challenges and dark nights of the soul as well as your growth, determination and successes. I honor the light that exists within each and every one of you. Namaste.

Finally, I want to honor **the source of all inspiration, light and goodness** that exists in my heart and throughout the entire universe. I know that your hand guided my hand through this process and I feel your support in me, through me and as me. I am so grateful for your infinite Love and Grace.

Contents

PAGE 9

Introduction
Why I wrote this book.

PAGE 12

Symbol Meanings
The meaning of symbols found throughout this book.

PAGE 13

Preface
What is feng shui? And why should you apply it to yourself?

PAGE 17

CHAPTER 1

Abundance and Prosperity
The definitions of abundance and prosperity mean much more than simply financial wealth. Broaden your definition and reap the rewards.

PAGE 31

CHAPTER 2

Passion and Romance
Become whole to attract a whole partner. Invite love into your life and realize that it's on its way.

PAGE 55

CHAPTER 3

Fame: How you are seen in the world
It's not necessarily about being famous. Put the right message into the world so people see you how you truly want to be seen.

PAGE 75

CHAPTER 4

Career and Service
Define what you want and make it your job to find your dream job.

PAGE 99

CHAPTER 5

Health and Balance

Tune into the principles of balance, harmony and flow to manifest vibrant health mentally, physically, spiritually and energetically.

PAGE 119

CHAPTER 6

Family and Past

Your past affects your present. Let go of bygone events and forgive to move freely into your ideal future.

PAGE 137

CHAPTER 7

Creativity and Future

Remember to think like a child to stimulate your creativity, dream big and create a blueprint for your success.

PAGE 155

CHAPTER 8

Wisdom and Self-Awareness

Access your authentic Self and your inner wisdom to know yourself better.

PAGE 175

CHAPTER 9

Faith and Benefactors

Help is out there for you. Identify the helping hands around you and have faith that you can create anything you want.

PAGE 189

Epilogue: How to read this book

Now that you've finished reading, consider doing it again—backward.

Introduction

Why I wrote this book

I woke up one day a few years ago with chronic back pain. My back hadn't felt good for some time, but there was no more denying it. It just wasn't going away. I was having a hard time being positive while I was in pain, and it took everything I had to get through those days. I realized ultimately that it wasn't about the pain itself, but more about what was happening underneath, inside me. Just like when a light on your car dashboard indicates a problem, it isn't necessarily the dashboard light that is broken, but more likely something else "under the hood."

There were some things in my life at the time that I had left unaddressed, and getting help for this pain was one of them. Finally, I could no longer let things stay as they were. I realized that I had been avoiding getting help for the back pain for a couple of reasons.

First, I was afraid of finding out something I didn't want to hear, like that I had a tumor in my back, or a herniated disc, or a life threatening or debilitating illness. And like many people I know (and several people I am related to), I chose to simply do nothing about it instead.

The other concern was that I didn't feel as though I had the extra money to pay for whatever the experts might find wrong or their prescribed course of treatment. As I examined this more deeply, I realized that I was playing an old story in my mind, which was that *I didn't have enough* to do anything about it. Underneath this idea was the thought that I couldn't have everything in my life be good all at the same time. If one area of my life was going well, it was inevitable that another part would be suffering—or so I thought. Then I fell in love with the woman who would become my wife.

In the midst of falling in love, I realized some important things. The first was that I wanted my best self to emerge. I didn't want to bring anything less than into my relationship because I valued it so highly, and I wanted my best self to be a foundation of our relationship. I made a promise that I wanted to keep: that I would always bring my best self forth. Then I asked myself, how could I make this possible?

In thinking about other parts of my life, I feel that I have a proven track record of success. One of the key ingredients for this success is that I can make things happen if I know what I'm aiming at. The only downside was that in the past, I generally found that as I was able to create success in one part of my life, inevitably another part suffered. I didn't like this idea that one part had to suffer in order for another area to flourish. It felt like a form of poverty thinking; that somehow there wasn't enough to go around. It reminded me of what I thought the world was like when I was growing up, and I decided that I had had enough.

I hypothesized what might happen if every part of my life was flourishing: win-win in all areas. And as I imagined it, a picture started to emerge, and I liked it. I began taking steps one at a time to address the parts of my life that weren't feeling balanced, that scared me, or were screaming for my attention.

I soon realized that things were shifting quickly in a positive direction. I found that the things I had been scared of were losing power, and my life was quickly starting to look like the one I had envisioned for myself. (I think that having someone else in my life that wanted to live the same way helped.) Then I started incorporating more and more of these tips and practices into work with my coaching clients and workshops, and finally created a workshop outline entitled "You Can Have It All."

People often aim at improving one area of their life, say their finances, at the expense of another area, like their relationship. My goal with the workshop was to see what could happen if we aim at the entire picture of our life at the same time. Could we step into having it all? I believe the answer is yes.

I have been living these principles and sharing them with others for as long as I have known about them, and as long as they remain effective tools, I will continue to share them. At the beginning of this year, I made a pact with myself that I began to share with others:

No more settling for "meh," "not bad," or "just ok." Let's seek to create space for more joy, better health, better sex and more abundance in all areas of our creative and personal lives. I wish you all of your wishes, and my hope is that this book will show you how to manifest them all.

And so it is...

Symbol Meanings

YIN YANG [BALANCE]
The universal symbol for balance. For our purposes, the light half represents everything you can experience with your five senses in the physical world. The dark half represents everything you feel with your intuition, i.e. your gut feelings.

EYE OF KANALOA [HUNA PRINCIPLE]
A Hawaiian symbol of healing. The root translation of Kanaloa means the great peace or the great stillness. The pattern represents the web of life; the symbolic connection of all things to each other. Generates subtle energy known as Ki in Hawaiian.

LOTUS FLOWER [HARMONY]
Meditating on the lotus brings harmony into all aspects of our being, within and without. The lotus is known for producing beauty (the flower) out of something ugly (the mud), which symbolizes our human struggles of taking something difficult and making it into something beautiful.

WAVE [FLOW]
Feng shui is about how to create more flow in our lives. The wave represents the flow of the river of life. How we allow that flow and how we navigate the river directly affects our experience.

Preface

Ever heard of feng shui? In a word, the concept means balance. In a sentence, it refers to the balance of energy within a space. If you're thinking that feng shui means moving your stuff around, you're right; that's the most well-known form of this concept. But there's a point at which our outer environment stops having a profound effect; it's really your inner self that allows the good energy you're welcoming into your home to affect you, so it makes sense that the definition of feng shui can easily be applied to another environment: You.

That's what this book is about—feng shui for your "inner house," or the application of traditional feng shui principles to your intellect, emotions, energetic body and physical body; in other words, to your mental, emotional, spiritual and physical sides.

If you would like an image, picture a small *mental* energy center around your head, a small *emotional* energy center around your heart and a larger *spiritual* energy center outside of your entire body. The energy center of your head represents your thoughts and intentions. The energy center of your heart represents the power that fuels your intentions. The energy center around your body regulates how much energy you draw to yourself at each moment. Each of these energy systems (as well as anything you ingest) influences and affects your physical body.

Inner feng shui is the idea of balancing all sides of yourself using the same three-step process you would apply to your outer spaces like your home, office and car. The three steps are: declutter, organize, and beautify.

Why should you feng shui yourself from the inside out? If certain areas of your life aren't progressing in a positive direction, you may be stuck. If you find that your romantic life isn't progressing, your finances aren't progressing, or you don't feel good or healthy in your skin and you keep coming up against the same spiritual lessons over and over, consider this: the inner reflects the outer and the outer reflects the inner. Cleaning house internally is a big step toward making space to allow what you want to flow to you. By applying the three-step process of decluttering, organizing, and beautifying to your energetic and physical self, you clear the way for the grandest vision of your life to become reality. It's an attitude: you *can* have it all.

How do you get it all? It's a process that requires honest inner digging. Some people believe that we get what we aim at, big or small, right or wrong. Our intentions direct our thoughts and actions toward our goals like arrows that fly toward their target. What happens if you aim at one portion of your life, such as work, but not others, like your health or relationships? It's likely that at some point you will have to stop what you're doing (being a workaholic) to help bring your life back into balance. This creates a win-lose outcome. But if you conceive of the bigger picture of your life and aim at it in its entirety at one time, you may be surprised at what is possible.

That's not to say you have to work on everything at once; you don't. Simply keeping the bigger picture in mind as the backdrop behind everything you do creates a win-win situation where all your needs are met, and it sets the stage for waking up in a more balanced tomorrow. What you excavate by doing the internal digging creates clarity of the vision you want for yourself, and what you need to do to get it becomes crystal clear. Once you're clear, you can manifest everything on your wish list.

With that in mind, this book is designed to lead you on a journey through the nine feng shui areas of life (Abundance & Prosperity, Passion & Romance, Fame & How You Are Seen in the World, Career & Service, Health & Balance, Family & Past, Creativity & Future, Wisdom & Self-Awareness, and Faith & Benefactors) and encourage you to reflect on how those parts of your life currently feel. These areas are part of a westernized system of feng shui known as Black Sect feng shui, and they relate to something called the Bagua map. This map is generally applied to a home or property, but in this case, we're navigating a path to your best you.

My feng shui master was Hawaiian and always included teachings from the ancient Hawaiian Huna secrets in his feng shui classes (huna means secret). He later created the Tibetan Hawaiian Feng Shui Foundation where I was trained. There are many crossovers between the principles of Huna and how they relate to energy and intention, which we will explore along with the feng shui principles in this book.

If the actions presented in this book feel good to you: start now. If they feel overwhelming: stop, and resume later. Sometimes a little bit at a time feels really good. Break the process down into bite-sized chunks and create your own path. Your ideal life is waiting for you and you can get there at a pace that feels just right to you. Let's get started.

Abundance and Prosperity

"The well of Providence is deep. It's the buckets we bring to it that are small."

— Mary Webb

THE HIGHEST GOOD PRINCIPLE

I think that many people in life are concerned that if they get what they really want, something bad will happen. W.W. Jacobs warned in his 1902 short story *The Monkey's Paw*: "Be careful what you wish for, you may receive it." The story was a horror tale, and the warning may stick in the back of our minds from childhood: if we receive something we really desire, someone could take it away, our friends might

Feng Shui principle

There are seven ancient Hawaiian Huna secrets as taught by their shamans (Kahunas). One is Kala, which means *There are no limits*. The idea behind this and the Mary Webb quote is that all limitations are set by people's own minds.

be jealous or we may feel guilty for having something while others suffer. But we don't have to think this way; as we can do with any thoughts that are no longer serving us, we can place them into a sacred fire of our own choosing, allowing them to be released

Color your world

The best colors for abundance and prosperity are deep purples, grounding golds, vibrant reds and grand greens. Think of the celebrations of Mardi Gras, the colors of the fall harvest and ceremonies of royalty.

once and for all.

In feng shui, we talk about intentions being the seeds that grow into the gardens of our experience. My feng shui master always said that we are allowed to ask for anything we can imagine, anything under the sun, and to never set limits to our desires. He also tempered this by saying that we can ask for anything we desire because we always add the phrase: "…as long as it is for our highest good and the highest good of others." This is like a spiritual or energetic insurance policy that can help allay the worries that stem from dreaming big. (The section **Highest Good of All**, pg. 24, explains this concept even further.)

Prosperity and abundance are often thought of as money, and having lots of it. Some people think of monetary wealth as abundance, while others think of health as abundance or a relationship as abundance. Those ideas seem to be hinting at a bigger picture, which is the good life—*all* areas of your life. The good life is the concept that you can have it all. Why choose? Why have a life where your career is thriving at the expense of your health, or have financial gain at the expense of your relationship? If you get what you focus on, why not conceive of a win-win scenario where you can aim at all of it and have it all? If it's overwhelming to focus on all the areas at once, then focus on one section at a time and the rest will come.

Don't put limits on your manifestations

Now that you're thinking about your specifics, don't put any limits on them. It's funny how sometimes people put so many limits on their beliefs before they even get started—sometimes even on their fantasies. The tree is the symbol for wealth in feng shui. They say your branches can only grow as high as your roots are deep. If you can't dream big, how can you receive big?

CLARIFY YOUR INTENTIONS

The first thing to do is create a clear image of what prosperity and abundance is for you. For example, let's say you feng shui the prosperity corner in your home and a few days later you find $20 in the street. Does that mean it's working? Technically, you have more money than you had before, but if you don't have a clear vision of what you're aiming at to begin with, then you won't know when you've received it. See if you can figure out how you will know you have accomplished your intentions. Picture it in your mind's eye. See the cast of characters who are present. Being specific about your intentions can allow you to track your progress to your goal.

Feng shui is about balance in all of its forms, especially in regard to your intentions. This means addressing all nine areas of life, not simply focusing on one area like wealth. If you were working out, it wouldn't make sense to use just one arm to lift a dumbbell every day. You would look funny, and you would hardly be in shape. The same is true when we define abundance or prosperity to simply mean wealth. See if you can expand your definition to include the idea of having the good life—health, wealth and happiness, or whatever the good life means to you.

A lot of people focus on just getting money, but then have no idea what to do once they have it. Studies show that more often than not, when people win the lottery, they eventually go broke or end up in a worse situation than before. It's not about just getting money, but also the wisdom of how to handle it. If you haven't healed your family area and your past, you might get big chunks of money, but you're constantly paying down debts you've accumulated. It's like having a hole in your bucket of wealth and before you can even count what you've brought in, you have pieces taken off the top.

Each of the nine areas of life needs to be addressed so you don't create an imbalance in your manifesting.

THE MAGIC WORDS

Let's imagine for a second that our words are powerful. Imagine that the thoughts we think and the words we say could be taken literally by some force, some presence that exists in our lives. Would this change the words you use when you are making your requests of the unknown and the infinite? For example, have you ever noticed that some people (let's call them the "just enough" people) always seem to have just enough to cover their monthly expenses, and no more? These people are constantly praying to just have enough to cover their bills. They are imagining their bills being paid and they are putting extra wattage of intention behind it by getting their whole heart involved. *Please. Let. Me. Have. Enough. This. Month.* This is the message that is being sent out like a radio signal to attract a "like match", and so it is.

In feng shui, you can't pick up something new unless you put down what you are holding onto. It's almost like a garden full of weeds—there's no room for anything new to grow. So the first stage of making space is to declutter; in this case, decluttering your mind from thoughts of "just

Pitfalls: Guilt and fear

Are guilt and fear keeping you from receiving what you want? Everything you have been asking for might be right at your door, waiting to be invited in, but those emotions may be indications that there are subversive thoughts keeping you from receiving what you say you want.

From a universal perspective, if you get what you have asked for but you feel guilty for receiving it, the vibration of guilt may send out a message that you are being harmed—a big red flag. Imagine that the universe is functioning from a neutral place of love and compassion. It would never want to see you harmed in the process of bringing you what you desire, and it might just be waiting for you to work out your guilt issues around receiving before you can fully receive what you are asking for.

If opportunities in your life are like water flowing to your front door, then fear is like a cold front freezing that water into ice. Fear literally constricts our blood vessels and slows down the flow of blood in our body. The message your body sends is to slow everything down or stop it until the danger is gone.

Both of these conditions seem to come from an imbalance in thought. A thought that **If I receive this, then someone or something else will not have enough, or will judge me for having it.** How can you put some space around these thoughts to include the possibility that if you receive what you ask for, it may benefit you and also those around you?

enough-ness." But nature abhors a vacuum. If you don't put something new in place of the old thought, similar useless thoughts are likely to pop back up, rendering your decluttering work a waste of time. So what are two of the most powerful words you can plant in the garden of your mind? The magic words *or more*.

You don't even have to change what you are asking for, but the invitation is to stay open to receiving that which you believe you need, or more. So the next time you are asking to receive "just enough work" to cover all of the bills you have coming up, see if you can make a little space for grace to add a little extra into your coffers.

WIN-WIN

In the old paradigm of wealth, people needed to accumulate wealth in order to have power, create status and fulfill aspects of the ego that would make them feel a sense of accomplishment. Throughout history, they accomplished this by doing whatever it took to achieve the vision or dream. The journey may have included stepping on people along the way and doing things that they knew, on some level, were wrong. These are examples of achieving personal gain at the expense of others, which makes achieving the goal feel empty. These actions are win-lose.

When I was twelve years old, our school asked us to raise money for a local charity. We were encouraged to go door to door and collect money for the cause. I don't know if I was very good at convincing people or if it was people's inherent generosity of spirit, but I ended up with a couple hundred dollars when all was said and done. We kept a paper record of our donations, but there was no oversight. I looked at the money and I instantly had a thought: if I kept the money, no one would know.

At that time, I was playing a lot with remote controlled cars. I went to the store and bought myself new gold painted hubcaps and wheels for my car. These were things I never would have bought with my own money. Two of my friends were jealous of my newly "tricked out" car. I had accomplished my goal. I thought it would make me feel better about myself, but it didn't.

I went to my mom and told her what I had done. She helped me try to return the items to the store, but they wouldn't take them back. I repaid every penny I had taken by emptying my savings from the bank. Years of odd jobs, birthdays and holidays…gone in a flash. I learned an invaluable lesson about money, and about win-lose scenarios. I had a win in one department (looking cool) but a lose in another (feeling badly for not being in integrity with myself.) I certainly wasn't perfect from that age on, but I definitely got the lesson that day.

What I learned is that this form of success (win-lose) is both unsustainable and dissatisfying. Why do you think so many of the wealthiest people become philanthropists? They have accomplished the desires of their ego and learned that it's more satisfying to empower others than to take from them. This is the shift from a win-lose paradigm to a win-win.

With a win-lose scenario, I have to take from you in order for me to benefit. With a win-win, as I benefit, I uplift the community around me. True abundance and prosperity benefits the greater good—you and everyone around you. Money sometimes has a bit of a fickle nature; it wants to know why you want it to come into your life. If you can expand your reasons for wanting this wealth and abundance (to create something, to help family and friends, to inspire others to what is possible) to include something deeper than the surface reasons (to have stuff), then perhaps it will come more quickly and stay longer. It will also make your story feel good to everyone who hears it, which goes beyond win-win into a win-win-win paradigm.

HIGHEST GOOD OF ALL

My grandfather was an incredibly successful businessman. He was a giant in the publishing industry, and his work on the ad council led him to meet everyone from heads of business to presidents. Every night before we ate dinner, I remember him saying the words, "May we be ever mindful of the needs of others."

Conscious capitalism

The win-win philosophy can be applied not only to your personal life and yourself, but to your work, too. The key is to be conscious of every professional decision and its impact on yourself, your business and the world around you. The conscious capitalism model is built on three core principles:

Deeper Purpose Recognizing that every business has a deeper purpose than merely profit maximization, a Conscious Business is clear about and focused on fulfilling its deeper purpose.
Stakeholder Model A Conscious Business focuses on delivering value to all of its stakeholders and works to align and harmonize the interests of customers, employees, suppliers, investors, the community and the environment to the greatest extent possible.
Conscious Leadership In a Conscious Business, management embodies conscious leadership and fosters it throughout the organization. Conscious leaders serve as stewards to the company's deeper purpose and stakeholders, focusing on fulfilling the company's purpose, delivering value to its stakeholders and facilitating a harmony of interests, rather than on personal gain and self-aggrandizement. Conscious leaders cultivate awareness throughout their business ecosystem, beginning with themselves and their team members, and moving into their relationships with each other and other stakeholders.

—From consciouscapitalism.com

In order for something to truly embody the principles of win-win, you must keep it in mind as you set out to accomplish your goals. How would getting my desires fulfilled impact others? In Black Sect feng shui, we always temper our desires with the phrase "for the highest good of all people concerned." This acts like an energetic insurance policy, a safety net or a guiding principle. It gives you permission to ask for whatever you want; the caveat is that it's for your highest good and the highest good of all involved, so you can't ask for anything that's too much.

On the surface, some of life's opportunities might look as if they're for your benefit, but later you may find that the look was deceiving. We never know why things work out as they do until we look through the glasses of hindsight. If we can begin to trust and intend our way through life that *everything* is functioning for a higher good, then we can relax and navigate the waters of opportunity with a renewed confidence and faith that all is as it should be.

THANK YOU IN ADVANCE

We have become accustomed to saying thank you after good things happen in life. It is polite, but it also feels good. So what happens if you start acting as if good things are already happening…before they happen? What if you begin to say thank you in advance, anticipating all of the good things that are on the way? Not only would you feel good from saying thank you, but you're putting "out there" that good things are coming, which may even help you create a self-fulfilling prophecy. Saying thank you sets a powerful intention for future success, and that intention starts now.

TITHING: GIVING BACK TO OUR SOURCE

They say the fastest way to get anything in life is to give it away, because you can't give away something you don't have. Sometimes we have to give in order to receive. One way to give back is through the process of tithing. Many people associate the process of tithing with the church or other religious institutions; what many people don't know is that farmers originally inspired the process.

Farmers noticed that if they harvested their entire crop annually, every few years there was a "down year," resulting in no crops. They found that by simply returning 10% of their crops to the soil that there were no down years. This is one of the founding principles of sustainability: keep 90% for yourself and give 10% back. This principle also applies to our lives. It's like the goose that laid the golden egg; if you get greedy and take too much, it stops.

The church adopted tithing because it's a business and it wants to survive, but the church is a metaphor for whatever helps you in your life. It doesn't matter what the thing is, give to something that sustains you in the world in some way. This could be a school, a spiritual community or a charity. It could be children, the environment or the arts. Give back of yourself in some way. If you feel moved to donate a portion of your paycheck, then do. If you prefer to give your time or your skills, that can be a beautiful thing and just as meaningful or more so than a monetary donation. As you give to something that represents your own source of inspiration and opportunity, the same invisible energy will always be there for you as well.

One afternoon about 12 years ago, a friend called and invited me to coffee. He asked me what was going on in my life and I told him that I was struggling. He listened intently as I shared with him all the ways in which I was having a hard time. At the end of our conversation he gave me a $100 bill. I was flabbergasted. He told me that a friend had done the same thing to him once and he wanted to pay it forward. He urged me to do the same thing one day when I felt moved to. I will never forget his kindness and I always remember his words.

I've experimented in many different ways with tithing through the years. I've given money and I've given my time. I've given to charities that I believe in: ones that build houses for those in need and those that create clean, safe water, or plant trees in areas that were devastated.

Inverse Tithing

There is a thought that if 10% is good, then 20% must be better. Or 50%. Or 80%. In an effort to be viewed as generous, it's possible to almost become greedy in a way. If giving is good, then giving more is better. Whatever your reasons for wanting to give this much, inverse tithing can become dangerous. That's when you give away 90% and only keep 10% for yourself. You may not feel worthy or deserving of receiving anything. You get something and immediately give it away. If someone gives you something, you immediately try to figure out how you can repay them.

For a while, this was me. I loved the feeling of giving so much that sometimes I kept doing it, even to my own detriment. I'd give money but then have to borrow for rent. I would donate so much of my time that I ended up not leaving enough time for paid work. And there were times that I was so exhausted that I wasn't of use to anyone.

If you do this, you too may become depleted and then have no choice but to ask for help. Imagine if you were a farmer and you gave 90% of your crop back to the soil. You would only have 10% left to sell, and then most of your work that year would go to waste. The soil doesn't need more than 10% to be sustainable, so challenge whether your desire to constantly give more is coming from a balanced place. (I'm not talking about philanthropy; if all of your needs are being met, then feel free to be as generous as you want. The information on inverse tithing is focused more on people who are struggling and feeling that they have to do more in order to get more, or to feel good about themselves.)

I've given to yoga studios, temples and the arts. I've given publicly and anonymously. And I've always been provided for—always and in all ways. Does it have anything to do with my tithing? Since I don't know for sure, it feels better to believe that it does than that it doesn't. It has always felt good to give and I do it as much for me as I do for others.

ONCE YOU GET IT, ENJOY IT AND HONOR WHAT GOT YOU THERE

Sometimes we arrive at our goal and without pausing for more than a second, we're instantly thinking of our next goal. But you may be forgetting how hard you've worked and all of the effort that went into accomplishing your dream. Take a pause and acknowledge your hard work, feel the feelings associated with getting what you worked for and allow yourself to really give yourself the accolades you deserve. This can certainly help build self-confidence for the future, and it will keep your days from blending together in a forgettable blur. If we don't take time to enjoy the fruits of our labor, we can lose sight of why we are doing this to begin with.

The good life is one where you have an abundance of health, wealth and happiness. When you have success and the fruits of that hard work come in, it is the happiness that will sustain you through the next cycle. The happiness will have long-term positive effects on your health as well.

Everything comes from the source and to the source it is returned, so be sure to honor those who helped you along the way. Honor the visible

EXERCISE: Test drive your life

Sometimes people wait for the stars to align before they take action. Others constantly act as if the thing they want is already happening, and then they allow themselves to catch up to what they commit to. But what if you aren't quite ready to take that leap of faith? Perhaps an easy way to dip your toe in the water is to test drive your life.

A lot of us make wish lists, lists of "somedays" and "what-if's." Places we want to travel. Things we want to buy. Relationships we hope will one day walk into our lives. They say destiny is where opportunity meets action, so where can you begin to take steps now, today?

If you want a new car, test-drive it to see how it feels. Don't just window shop, try on the dress or rings or shoes and see what the experience is like. Go to the open house. Price out the trip around the world. Something powerful happens when you take action and set things into motion.

Make a list of the eight things you most want to test drive in your life, and do it in order of priority within the next 40 days. Why eight? Eight is often thought of as a number that relates to abundance and prosperity. Why 40 days? It's the number that relates to a spiritual journey (think Noah on the Ark, Jesus in the desert or Buddha under the tree). If you want to keep a journal or make notes on the list of how the experiences feel as you complete each one, you can reflect on them later to remind yourself of the accomplishments and positive energy you manifested by "trying on" your ideal life.

allies (family, friends, community, spiritual leaders) and the invisible helping hands (your highest source, God, guardian angels or whatever you personally believe in). People will appreciate your thanks and will be more likely to help again in the future.

After sports teams win, they have a parade. It's a way of giving back to all of the fans that rooted for them along the way. Whether it's a party, a dinner or simply raising a glass in a toast, do something to honor the occasion with a celebration of your process. Celebrate, appreciate, rinse and repeat.

"Until one is committed there is hesitancy,
the chance to draw back, always ineffectiveness.
Concerning all acts of initiative (and creation),
there is one elementary truth,
the ignorance of which kills countless ideas
and splendid plans:
that the moment one definitely commits oneself,
then Providence moves too.
All sorts of things occur to help one
that would never otherwise have occurred.
A whole stream of events issues from the decision,
raising in one's favour
all manner of unforeseen incidents
and meetings and material assistance,
which no man could have dreamt
would come his way.
I have learned a deep respect
for one of Goethe's couplets:
'Whatever you can do, or dream you can, begin it.
Boldness has genius, power and magic in it.' "

—from The Scottish Himalayan Expedition, 1951
—W.H. Murray

Passion and Romance

❝Your task is not to seek for love, but merely to seek and find all the barriers within yourself that you have built against it.❞ — **Rumi**

BECOME WHOLE

We all want to be loved, and many of us will do just about anything to feel connected to love in some way. Some of these ways feel good and some of them leave us feeling dissatisfied. If a dynamic is imbalanced, we eventually move on until we find some new external source of our inspiration or happiness. If we seek for this source outside of ourselves, we continue a paradigm

Feng Shui principle

"You must be a one before you can be a two." In numerology, the number one comes before the number two. The metaphor in relationships is one where many of us try to find someone to "complete us," or someone that we can teach, fix or save. By becoming whole first, we can bypass co-dependence and instead build a partnership that is mutually uplifting and sustainable over the long haul.

 Color your world

The best colors for attracting love are passion colors. Luscious reds, vibrant pinks and energizing oranges all stimulate the right chakras. Passionate purples and grounding golds are also helpful. For milder love, choose a lighter shade, a pastel or an off white with a hint of color.

within which we are like love vampires, eternally destined to find our next fix—anyone to put out the inner burning of loneliness for awhile.

I used to be a love vampire. Having divorced parents led me to constantly seek attention. The attention felt really good, but it was never enough to truly satisfy my need, and as a result, I had many unrequited relationships. Eventually I realized it was a cycle that I needed to break. It was a children's book that finally helped me realize the importance of becoming whole myself before I got into a relationship. The book—Shel Silverstein's *The Missing Piece*—was written for kids, but is actually a perfect metaphor for relationships. In it, a circle with a missing piece is looking for someone or something to fill its hole, and is seeking something outside of itself to fill it. My interpretation: in life, most of us look outside of ourselves for missing pieces to fill our holes.

It's as if each of us wanders the earth with a glass of precious water. We come across someone who is thirsty

> **Take a look around your life**
>
> Are there any areas of shame surrounding your physical appearance, self-esteem, health or finances? If so, this shame might spill over into the relationship you are seeking. They are never going to be perfect, but if you can start tackling the work of rebalancing these parts of your life, you will feel better and that good feeling will carry over into your love relationships. Many of my friends have told me how attracted they are to people they see owning and working on their "stuff." Our baggage comes to light sooner or later, so why not start now?

and pour some of our water into their glass. It satisfies them, for a while. Or we are walking around empty, thirsty, and we do whatever it takes to get someone to pour some of their water into our glass. When we fall in love, we might pour the entire contents of our glass into our lover's glass in an effort to demonstrate our love. Sensing that our glass is empty, they might pour the entire contents back into our glass. And back and forth we pour and sip and spill from each other's glasses until we run out.

If we would simply stop for a moment and turn around, there is an infinite, energetic source available to us at any time. It's like a waterfall: abundant, ever flowing and infinite. All we need to do is draw inside and we can fill our own glass at will. If everyone became aware of their own inner source of infinite supply, it might completely transform the paradigm of relationships and their purpose in our lives.

As Steven Covey describes in his book *The Seven Habits of Highly Successful People,* we all move through different stages of dependence. When we're born, we're dependent on our parents. After the dependency stage, we are invited to become completely independent. From independence, we can move into a state of interdependence (when two whole people come together.) If we never become a whole person during the independence stage, when we connect with others, it creates a form of co-dependence where we look to the other person to complete us in some way. Whatever is unresolved in our past relationships becomes the baggage we bring with us from relationship to relationship.

This isn't to say we have to wait until we are in some idealized state of perfection before we can be with someone. Just like we don't throw away every item we own before we move (we don't completely start anew), the invitation is to only bring with us what is most important to us. This period of self-discovery before we call another person into our lives can help us to avoid bringing extra "stuff" to the table. We will always have lessons in life, but the more freedom we bring to the relationship, the more open we are to co-creating a beautiful life.

BREAK BAD PATTERNS

I've had clients complain to me that in relationships, they keep meeting the same person over and over again. If that's true for you, it might be time to do an inner feng shui cleanse. The common denominator in all of these relationships is *you*; perhaps you're putting something out there that keeps attracting the same situation. Do you have recurring thoughts about yourself that might be influencing the people you are attracting? For example, a woman in Karen Rauch Carter's book *Move Your Stuff, Change Your Life* kept saying she wanted a husband, over and over again. "I want to meet a husband." All she kept meeting were married men.

The first step is to recognize that you have a pattern. You may have no idea how you got there, but you know you don't like it and you want a way out. You may crawl around in the dark, but eventually you do what it takes and you will find a way out. The next time may be different.

As soon as you become aware of a pattern, see if you can watch the whole process like an outside observer. It's only by becoming aware of what we're doing that we can make a change. Once we have mastery at changing a pattern that is no longer serving us, we can avoid that pattern altogether.

There's a Hole in My Sidewalk

Autobiography in Five Short Chapters

By Portia Nelson

CHAPTER ONE

I walk down the street.
There is a deep hole in the sidewalk.
I fall in.
I am lost .... I am helpless.
It isn't my fault.
It takes forever to find a way out.

CHAPTER TWO

I walk down the street.
There is a deep hole in the sidewalk.
I pretend that I don't see it.
I fall in again.
I can't believe I am in this same place.
But, it isn't my fault.
It still takes a long time to get out.

CHAPTER THREE

I walk down the same street.
There is a deep hole in the sidewalk.
I see it is there.
I still fall in ... it's a habit ... but my eyes are open.
I know where I am.
It is my fault.
I get out immediately.

CHAPTER FOUR

I walk down the same street.
There is a deep hole in the sidewalk.
I walk around it.

CHAPTER FIVE

I walk down another street.

YOUR WORDS GIVE YOU AWAY

I have a dear friend who several years ago was diagnosed with a severely advanced form of cancer. She went through several rounds of chemo, lost all of her hair and spent her entire savings (and then some) going through treatment. She rehabilitated by getting regular acupuncture, changing her diet and taking a steady regimen of Chinese herbs. Today she is cancer free. It is miraculous to see and she is an inspiration to many.

When I first met her, it was rare to go through a conversation or a meal without her telling a story that started with "when I had cancer" or "having been through cancer" or "the people who helped me through cancer." It is truly a miracle that she is still with us. I admire her spirit, her friendship and everything she has taught me. In this case, she has demonstrated how parts of our story may be the lens through which we see everything in our lives.

I can tell a lot about a client from the way they talk about themselves, the important people in their life and their circumstances. I can tell if they are positive or negative, if they are hopeful or resigned and if they are telling themselves an old story of past pain.

I have clients who speak about wanting to find love, but the second they talk about the men in their life, their whole energy changes. I hear a new tone or see body language, but most of all hear negative words about how evil their ex was. Their words indicate that they are still incredibly angry or resentful or both. And even though these people didn't feel angry, they were still upset at something that had happened that they were unwilling or unable to understand, accept or forgive. Unresolved feelings toward an ex or parent can create an energetic barrier to receiving love from someone new.

WATCH YOUR LANGUAGE

How you talk to yourself is immensely important. Words are *very* powerful. They help us create the stories we tell ourselves about ourselves. These stories can help us feel empowered and confident, or foolish and unlovable. As my dear friend and acting coach Warner Loughlin likes to say, "Choice affects perception and perception affects choice." We have a choice in how to perceive things. Through our change in perception, we may change the opportunities that present themselves.

Perhaps you notice certain words you use to describe yourself or your current circumstances. For example, there's a difference between feeling lonely and being alone. Loneliness implies some sort of lack. Perhaps a lack of connection to another person, to the community we are in, or to our own source. In this way, feeling loneliness becomes more of a burden. The invitation is to shift your perspective and to re-empower yourself.

The implication of feeling lonely is *I'm alone and I have no choice.*

Is there a way to rethink this by deciding that it *is* a choice? Try to experience what it feels like to say *I'm choosing to be alone because, at the moment, there's no one I want to be with.* Even if you are trying to get over someone, there's a difference between confidently knowing that the universe has your back and choosing to believe a disempowering story like *I couldn't go on a date even if I wanted to,* or *nobody likes me.*

This ties in perfectly with co-dependency. If someone isn't comfortable being alone, they are likely to attract another lonely person instead of a whole, integrated person choosing to be with a whole, integrated person. The loneliness feeling might be a precursor to self-sabotaging behavior—whether it's eating your way out of it, giving all of your power away, sleeping around or dating people you know are wrong for you.

So how do we break these patterns? Some people say a mantra to reconnect them to the source of their power and confidence. Others work at gathering evidence that they aren't alone by focusing on what they do have in their lives instead of what they don't have. In their case, it is changing a story about separateness, which ultimately is an illusion.

Whatever you think or say after the words "I AM…"is very powerful. See if you can change the story you tell yourself about yourself and the world around you will begin to change. I, myself, have experienced this. A few years ago, I noticed that whenever anyone would ask me how I was doing, I replied, "I'm OK. I'm not bad." That answer seemed to be socially acceptable. The conversation didn't last very long, and nobody got uncomfortable. Then I noticed that a friend of mine would answer that question with "I'm wonderful!" It made me wonder which created which? Did saying "I'm wonderful" create the day that way?

From then on, my reply to that question—on purpose—became "I'm wonderful! I'm excellent. Things are amazing." As soon as I started doing that, I noticed the parts of my life that already were those things, and by saying "I'm wonderful" or "I'm excellent," it usually directed my day toward having a wonderful experience.

INVITE LOVE INTO YOUR LIFE

Be your own best partner. Be willing to take yourself on a date, even if you're with friends. Go to the restaurants you might like to go on a date. Toast as if you are celebrating the love in your life. Put yourself in the environment of romance—watch your favorite romantic comedies, read poetry about love. Do what feels good to you.

Be aware of what you are putting out there. Are you putting out a vibration that is magnetic and drawing people in, or repelling and pushing people away? Think about someone who feels hopeless, lonely or bitter. Does that make you feel more drawn to them or pushed away?

Create an inner environment of hope, positivity and feeling good. Get a massage. Do Yoga. Play basketball or take Jiu Jitsu. Do things that make you feel good in your skin, feel good physically or feel confident. All of those things make you more magnetic.

Know what you want so you can articulate it to others. If you don't know what you like, go explore. Try bringing yourself fresh flowers from the farmer's market. Look at different types, smell them, get to know their names and meanings and then see how they feel in your house. A client in one of my *You Can Have It All* workshops told me that the number one thing she wanted in her life was a relationship. I gave her this task—

buying flowers for herself every week until someone else took over the job. Within a month, she started dating someone who did take over the job, and she is still dating him now.

You need to be able to articulate your needs and desires to someone when you're in a relationship, so start gathering information now so you can be prepared.

REALIZE THAT PASSION AND ROMANCE ARE ON THE WAY

I know we would all like to have evidence that things are happening, but it never seems to work like that. We never seem to have absolute certainty before we act. That's what a leap of faith is all about—we act and trust that the evidence will come later. You would never dig up the seeds you plant in your garden each night to see if they are growing. We must do our actions and then endure the unknown period between action and result.

One way to help with the in-between stage is to go inside and recognize that what you're manifesting is already on its way. Imagine someone emails you an attachment and you start to download it. You watch the progress bar and wait …1%, 30%, 75%. It's on its way, but watching the progress bar doesn't make it happen any faster. There's no way to see the "progress bar" when it comes to love, but you can start to notice little changes as your relationship "downloads."

Notice how people are responding to you in the world. Maybe someone notices something different about you, or you catch someone giving you a lingering look, or someone pays you an unexpected compliment. These are all signs that your inner seeds are taking root and sprouting. Your inner magnet is turned on, and it's only a matter of time before the evidence of a relationship comes into your experience.

GET OUT THERE AND DATE

When I first moved to Los Angeles, a psychic to the celebrities told me (as lovingly as possible) that I had no dating personality. He told me I was either on the path to marriage, or I was in the friend zone. To a degree, he was right. I put everyone into a category immediately and there was no gray area. So I started going out on dates—some with girls who were truly friends and some romantic dates. I was practicing and gathering information on what it was that I wanted. Soon it became easier for me to go beyond first impressions and see the person that was really there in front of me.

Dating is important in the process of finding love. It's up to you to decide if you feel comfortable dating one person at a time or multiple people simultaneously. If dating multiple people at once is within your comfort zone, it can be a great way to compare people in real time. A relationship coach named Pat Allen suggests that if you date one person, the pressure is on: it's all or nothing. With two people it's either/or. By dating three people at once, there's diversification, which is good for business and allows you to compare prospective partners in real time. Dating multiple people simultaneously requires a lot of honesty with you and with others. What are the rules? What's in bounds? What's off limits? How do you communicate enough to be respectful, but not so much that you feel like you're divulging too much information for everyone's comfort? It can be a tricky balance.

Everyone is going to create their own list of guidelines based on what makes them feel comfortable, but the key thing is to use consideration for another person's feelings. If you were the other person, what would you appreciate hearing about what you are doing?

Perhaps you will tell the other person that you are dating right now. You may decide to date a few people but without involving sex. That doesn't mean you can't have sex if you want to, but the general common knowledge is that sex complicates things. Obviously, as soon as something changes for you and you want to make a commitment with someone, communicate your desire and hopefully they feel the same way. If everyone involved has clear ideas of what they are agreeing to, then it can make for easier waters to navigate.

If you're with one person and you think they're fantastic and could be the one for you, it doesn't mean you need to force yourself to go out with other people. You don't have to torture yourself. Some people might have their head spin if they date more than one person at a time. Only you can know what works for you. If your tendency has been one way and it doesn't seem to be working, perhaps you might try taking a different approach. See how it feels.

PUT IT ON DISPLAY

It's important to be aware of what you are selling. This helps people understand what agreements you are inviting them into. Do you want to get married? Have a long-term committed relationship? Have a fling? Have several flings? At their core, relationships come down to agreements between two people. *I would like to make this agreement with you; are you willing?* The main way people become frustrated is if they think they have an understanding of what you want, and then come to understand that you actually want something different. You might feel nervous about stating the truth so quickly into your relationship. You may have to risk being judged for what you want or rejected because you aren't on the same page. With the person you are meant to be with, it won't matter. Even if it comes out clumsy, it's important to know and share the truth. It will come out at some point, and you can save a lot of time, money and heartache with being clear about your intentions up front.

The second way that this comes into play is with your physical attributes. Some people are self-conscious about their bodies, so they want to hide in some way. Others might like certain aspects of themselves, but want to distract from other aspects. This is normal. We want to be liked; we don't want to be rejected. But if you are selling friendship, then you will attract opportunities for friends. And if you want romance, part of it is allowing the other person to really see you to decide if they like what they see.

One client told me that she liked her body, but didn't want to be with someone if that was that was the only thing they were interested in. To her, somehow having someone interested in her physically implied that they were shallow and couldn't also respect her mind, her dreams or her feelings. We discussed her ultimate goal as being with someone who liked her on all levels. I asked her if she was willing to consider that by hiding, she might be putting out a confusing signal. She considered how she could envision a win-win partnership that included physical attraction, but that it wasn't the only factor in the relationship. She found an outfit that made her feel good in her skin, that showed off her body in a way that she felt comfortable with. The very next night, she got attention from some girl friends wanting to know why she was dressed this way (they weren't used to it, but they liked it) and several guys who paid attention to her throughout the evening. She called me the next day incredibly excited. Putting herself out there made it easier for people to see her in a romantic way.

S.E.X. = SACRED ENERGY EXCHANGE

My teacher Yasuhiko used to refer to sex as a sacred energy exchange, and it's important to be careful who you choose to exchange energy with. As it turns out, there may be scientific rationale behind this concept. A book called the *Secret Life of Plants* by Peter Tompkins and Christopher Bird was written about the controversial work of Cleve Backster, who founded the CIA's polygraph unit after World War II.

Backster's work focused on the subject of biocommunication, in which he experimented with the effect that human consciousness had on plants. The phenomena is now known as the Backster Effect. Backster hooked up the leads of a lie detector to thousands of plants. He went on to attach the leads to cells including those of amoeba, yeast, mold, blood and sperm.

What he discovered is that there is a communication system between thoughts and these cells. The most surprising discovery was that this affect could be produced over distance, which explains why twins have been known to feel what their sibling is feeling at the same moment, even if they are far away. Their cells are literally in communication with each other.

The impact of his findings means that our thoughts can influence the reactions of cells—ours and the people we come into contact with.

Imagine then that these cells, influenced by our thoughts, are being passed back and forth within our saliva and other fluids that we may exchange. If you are a generally happy person and you have been making out or making love with someone who is going through a major depression, it is possible that there could be an impact on your own moods. Picture a radio signal that is

More on sex

Everyone has urges, but they don't always reflect our deeper wisdom or knowing what is best for our highest good. If you feel connected with someone and it feels right, then celebrate that connection, but know that regardless of your intentions and communication that it will very likely change things for you both. It may change things for better or for worse. It might make one of you more attached. It might change how you feel about the other people you are dating. Some people say that sex clouds their thinking and the way they perceive the other person. The invitation is to put some space between you and the decision to act on your urge. See if a little restraint ends up giving you more clarity and perspective. Maybe just make out a little and trust that if the connection is strong, it will be there the next time you see them.

In the recommendation of dating multiple people, I don't recommend sleeping with them all at the same time unless you're telling everyone and being safe about it. There's an electrochemical and energetic set of connections that are built during sex, and if you have multiple partners it can create the potential for cross wiring. Perhaps you might need some sexual healing after a long period of dissatisfaction. Do what feels good for the part of you that knows you best. It might be that your short-term desires don't meet your long-term goals. Check in and see.

being exchanged between that person and all of their cells, which are now floating around your inner bloodstream. This radio signal is being affected by thoughts, some of which may not even be your own. This could explain the insight with mothers and their children in what we call "mother's intuition." Consider this the next time you decide to "exchange energy" with someone. There may be a longer lasting impact of their energy on your own than you ever thought was possible.

HOW TO RECOGNIZE A GOOD CATCH, A LIFE-PARTNER OR A SOUL MATE

There are usually two factors to consider when you're sizing up a potential partner: The *idea* of what you want, and the *feelings* you get from being with that person. No matter how much time we spend in the mental process of figuring out if the person meets our needs, usually the feeling we have about them is right. It can be tricky to navigate. Perhaps the important thing is to build in road markers or signs that allow you to know if you're headed toward the right direction or arriving at your destination.

Conventional wisdom is never to go grocery shopping when you're hungry. You could end up with a bunch of junk food, things that go to waste, or you may not get everything you need for the recipe you plan to cook. In that same sense, it might be important to have a list of ingredients that go into the relationship you wish to cultivate. Create a list of essential ingredients (deal breakers—your absolute must-have's) that will help you on your journey. Along the way, stay open to discovering anything that you feel might enhance the recipe in some way (preferences.) See if you can stay open to being surprised, delighted or open to the idea of changing your mind. The goal is not to make the ideal meal, but to become a master chef. The more clear you get, the easier it will be to know if you are on the right track.

For me, identifying the woman who would eventually become my wife happened only after I became a master chef of what I wanted. We were friends for a couple of years first, and didn't look at each other romantically. Then, one day, the universe intervened in New York over lunch. Neither of us expected it, but what came from it was magical. It was during that lunch that we talked about what we really wanted out of our lives, and realized we both wanted the same things. It was essential to me to tell her exactly what I was looking for. Instead of shying away and playing coy, I was super direct about marriage, kids and career (the big picture). Everything seemed to line up with both of our wants. Thanks to this conversation (and the help of her Aunt Phyllis), we were shaken out of "friendship mode" and invited to look at each other on a deeper level. I'm so grateful that we did.

RELATIONSHIPS NEED TO EVOLVE

I think some people view relationships as a sort of finish line, as if once they cross the finish line by finding a mate, they've won something. Their relationship status has changed and all that's left is to "put it on Facebook." This is an illusion, but we seem willing to believe it.

We see this in the movies. It's all about the meeting, the obstacles that keep our lovers apart, and the couple coming together at the end. We love to see people reunite at the end of the film, but then what? We know what happens "When Harry Met Sally," but what happens a few years later? Relationships are living, breathing things. They need to be fed, have enough space to grow and they need certain conditions to be met, or they will die.

Some people have green thumbs when it comes to plants. They know that plants take pruning, that they need to re-potted so that they have room to continue growing, and that they need sunlight, water and loving care to thrive. This process is in harmony with three important feng shui principles: decluttering, reorganizing and beautifying. We must remove what is no longer serving us. We must organize our space to serve a clear purpose. And then we must add in elements that support these things coming into our lives.

The same is true for relationships. We are constantly growing and shifting as individuals. The things that serve us through certain stages of our life change, expand and fall away. We must let go of what is no longer serving us in order to make room for something new to enter into our lives. Our needs change over time. We might find that we need to organize our lives around our changing desires. During one stage, we might seek our fortunes or travel the world. During our next stage, we might crave nesting and having a family. Once we decide what our new vision is, we might need support in achieving these goals. It could be finding ways to stay positive through the unknown time between vision and manifestation. It could be knowing that we have the emotional support of our loved ones, or it could be nurturing and physical touch.

There are different theories about the phases of a relationship. The general consensus is that after the initial honeymoon phase ends, there's a struggle that ends with a choice either to deepen the love or to part ways. Studies have shown that both Generation X (Gen X) and Generation Next (Gen Y) seem to have a tendency to fall in love, then to leave as soon as things get tough. Some people call this honeymoon surfing. They move from one relationship that feels good—until it doesn't—to the next, continually seeking the honeymoon stage with someone new.

In my 20's, I was a honeymoon surfer. Because my parents were divorced, I was constantly on the lookout for reasons why the relationship wouldn't work. As soon as things started to look rough, I used it as an excuse to end the relationship.

The honeymoon stage of a relationship lasts for a limited period of time. Some say that this stage lasts for six months to a year; the exact amount of time is probably different for every couple. After the honeymoon stage is over, people tend to go into the power struggle stage, where both compete to see whose needs are going to be met. The way we handle these needs will ultimately inform our decision to stay together or to part ways.

So what is it that keeps relationships alive? First, we need to make space for each other. Making space for each other is an absolute necessity; in the past, I found myself smothering relationships because of a lack of trust. Doing so puts undue strain on the relationship and there's no way it can survive. If we can give our partner space, we will always have room for our relationship to grow. As much as there is comfort in knowing everything about our significant others, we must make space for the unknown. This is where spontaneity, newness and possibility live. This is what allows us to feel as we did when we were teenagers and didn't know what was coming next.

Second, in a world where there are many examples of relationships that have failed, it's important to have examples of relationships that work. In observing these relationships, we don't have to emulate the way they look, but we can identify the principles that seem to make them work. I have two family friends, a couple that I've known since I was born, Miles and Judy. I always come back to thinking about them when I think of a great example of a relationship that works beautifully. At times when I was trying to see if a relationship that I was in at that time was truly right for me, I often used the principles that I saw in Miles and Judy's relationship as a way of gauging how much future potential mine had.

It was easy to see the love Miles and Judy have for each other. They also supported each other's evolution over time, and were always physically and verbally demonstrative of their love for each other. They were able to listen to each other, even during the hardest times. I noticed that they extended these same behaviors to their children, and I'm so impressed with the way their children have turned out. These principles are good for relationships in general, not just romantic ones.

The third thing that helps keep relationships alive are things that continually beautify our relationships. Appreciation goes a long way to making us feel loved. Affection and physical touch can have considerable health benefits and help us live a long time. Telling each other the truth is essential. When we no longer feel as though we can be honest with the person we love, our relationship with them dies a little.

See if you can identify what helps make a relationship thrive. Ask for what you need. Communicating your needs makes it more likely to be able to evolve together.

CLEAR BOUNDARIES

Sometimes when we're involved in a relationship, we have a tendency to lose ourselves. We may, out of love, start to compromise aspects of ourselves in an effort to please the other person. In this way, we may stop fueling the very qualities that made us attractive to each other to begin with. It's important to set boundaries around certain things.

A boundary can be a positive thing. It can help to clarify, protect or differentiate something from something it is not. In feng shui, it's important to set boundaries within certain areas of the house because they can interfere with the main purpose of a room. For example, having work in the bedroom lessens our ability to focus on rest or to connect to our lovers. We may do certain things out of convenience (like bringing a laptop to bed), but over time, we may find that our lover does not view the bed as a sacred space. We might bring our fights into bed and then no longer view it as a safe place. Or we could watch TV in bed and no longer view it as a passionate place.

Relationships start to have problems when other things take higher priority for an extended period of time. Thoughts about finances or our ability to provide might start to dominate our thoughts. We may be concerned with our health and our sense of how we feel in our own skin, or the needs and desires of our families and friends may challenge our own.

A boundary is about when to say yes and when to say no. We can say yes to every situation and then feel overtaxed. Or we might find ourselves in the habit of saying no before we even finish hearing what is being asked of us. There are ways to say yes to any situation, under certain circumstances. Regardless of what you say yes or no to, these small words can have huge impacts on the course of our relationships and how they feel along the way.

As we navigate through life, it's not that difficult to say no to something we don't want so we can say yes to something we do want. However, it can be very difficult to say no to things we do want to so we can say yes to something we *really* want. Making space can be scary, but doing so allows room for your deepest desires to flourish.

By placing strong boundaries around that which is most important to us, we can send a clear signal to everyone involved and keep everyone on the same page, including ourselves. As Steven Covey also said, "The main thing is to keep the main thing the main thing."

Exercise: The brain dump

One of my favorite exercises to do is something called the brain dump. It's where you literally take all of the thoughts in your head, shake them out and make sense of them. It can be particularly helpful when trying to clarify what you want in your dream job, dream apartment or dream relationship. The way it works is to ask yourself a question on a particular subject. When it comes to passion and romance, the question could be: what are the qualities that are most important to me in a long-term committed relationship?

PART ONE] Make the clay

The first thing to do is to make a list (without judgment or censoring yourself) of everything that is important to you. This is like making clay; you aren't judging what it looks like, you're just getting it out. Your list could consist of a range of items from the smallest thing (someone who likes the exact same cookies I do) to a large thing (someone who is close enough to be able to date.)

PART TWO] Shape the clay

Now that you have your initial list, look it over. Is it as clear as mud? Go line by line and make sure you are clear about each image. If it is vague, be more specific. If it is a negative, see if you can make it a positive. Make sure you are clear and succinct about what you are saying you want.

Hint: Sometimes it can be easier to figure out what you want by starting with a list of what you definitely **don't** want and then writing the reverse (i.e. **I want to stop attracting unavailable people** becomes **my preference is to be with someone who is available for me to be with them**.)

PART THREE] Make your sculpture

The last stage has two parts. First, put the list in order of priority. Go down your list and ask yourself if each item is a deal breaker (something you definitely must have), or a strong preference. A deal breaker might be **wants children**; a preference might be **over 6 feet tall.** Put an asterisk (*) next to each deal breaker. Then put a number from 1 to 10 next to each preference to rank how strongly it matters to you (1 being not at all to 10 being a very strong preference). You might find that they all are important, but see if, in relationship to each other, some matter more than others.

Second, rewrite your list. Place all the deal breakers up top and draw a line underneath them; these are conditions that your relationship **MUST** meet, without exception. Underneath the line, write the rest of the items on your list in sequence from most important to least important.

You now have a checklist that can be used to assess any potential suitor (or job, apartment or anything else you want to test to see if it meets your needs). Try it out; see if you can put an ex-boyfriend or ex-girlfriend through this system. It should start to become clear why things didn't work out.

I recommend that a dream relationship meet ALL of your deal breakers and at least 80% of your strong preferences. You can adjust your list as you see fit, but this is a great way of seeing specifically what works and what doesn't work for you about a situation you are unclear about. I shared this exercise with my cousin when she was dating several people, and it gave her instant clarity.

Fame and How you are seen in the world

"Your beliefs become your thoughts. Your thoughts become your words. Your words become your actions. Your actions become your habits. Your habits become your values. Your values become your destiny."

—Mahatma Gandhi

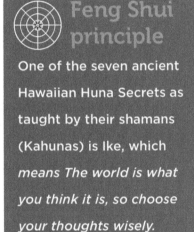

Feng Shui principle

One of the seven ancient Hawaiian Huna Secrets as taught by their shamans (Kahunas) is Ike, which *means The world is what you think it is, so choose your thoughts wisely.*

BE "THE SPOON" YOU WISH TO SEE IN THE WORLD

On the surface, it appears we are talking about being famous, and that is certainly one aspect of this area. The real thinking is on how you wish to be seen in the world. In order to make any significant change in life, you must change what you believe about yourself before recruiting others to support you in this belief.

In the movie *The Matrix*, Keanu Reeves's character, Neo, goes to see The Oracle to ask if he is "the One." While he's in the

Color your world

The best colors for fame are colors that attract attention: fiery reds, sizzling pinks and passionate oranges. Also helpful are reddish purples and electric yellows. Wear the colors that make you feel confident, passionate and ready to take on the world.

waiting room, he sees a child bending spoons with his mind. Neo picks up a spoon and attempts to use his own mind to bend the spoon in his hand. The child turns to him and says, "You think there is a spoon. In actuality, there is no spoon… it is *you* that must bend."

If the outer world is "the spoon" and you spend your time getting the world to change to fit what is inside of you, you might exhaust yourself. But if you change the way you see yourself and stand up for what you believe, the world will adapt itself to support your newfound belief. This is the definition of your reputation preceding you. Reputation, in this case, is how you wish to be perceived on all levels: physically, spiritually, mentally and emotionally.

In order to know what the world thinks of your "spoon," you have to know what you're putting out there, and how the people around you perceive what you're putting out there. In other words, what are you selling? What is the message you're currently selling to the world about yourself?

PUT THE RIGHT MESSAGE INTO THE WORLD

According to many child development experts, in order to develop in a healthy way, children need to be seen and heard. This need carries over to us in our adult life. Not feeling seen or heard by the people in our lives can contribute to low self-esteem, make us feel misunderstood, or worse, invisible. But how can we expect others to see us unless we see ourselves clearly? The first step is gaining awareness of how we are being seen in the world. This self-awareness is made possible by gathering feedback from others as to how they see us. One way to do this is to shine a light on the outer world and ask for feedback. Whatever message you put out will dictate the responses you get, so check in and see what message you're putting out there.

Some trucks have the words "How am I driving?" written on the back of them. There is a phone number you can call to give feedback if you see someone driving in a way that makes you want to speak up. You might wish you had a feedback line of how you are being perceived in the world, but the reality is that we all get feedback from the world on a daily basis. We just need to tune into what we're being told by others' comments, actions and reactions.

Is there anything you have heard about yourself over and over? Or have been asked regularly? Perhaps you keep getting the question "Is everything ok?" Upon further digging, you might find that people think something is going on with you or that you are sad. If you are sad, then you have to decide how you feel about people picking up on your sadness. If you are not sad, then you are faced with a choice. Simply dismiss this feedback, or dig a little deeper and see if there is any truth to these perceptions. You might be surprised what you learn about yourself.

I have a client who, at one point, was having trouble and expressing some frustration in either relationship or career. One of his closest friends told my client that he noticed a lot of anger coming from him; he said "You're coming across as super angry." It was very interesting because he had no idea that that's what he was putting into the world. There was something

" I love you, and because I love you,
I would sooner have you hate me
for telling you the truth than
adore me for telling you lies. "
—Mahatma Gandhi

about gathering information, even if it was something he didn't want to hear, that was important. Don't be afraid to ask for feedback from people, even if it pushes your buttons.

If you haven't noticed any patterns of what people have said about you, then you may need to dig a little deeper. Ask people directly what they think about you. Post a funny questionnaire on Facebook. Or send a direct letter or email to a trusted council of friends, co-workers and loved ones. Whatever you do, ask. [Warning: If you ask the question, be prepared to listen to the response.] If none of this feedback is clear or useful, there are workshops and courses that can give you insight into how you are perceived. Check with healing centers and yoga studios in your area, or look into programs offered at centers such as Esalen Institute (Big Sur, California), Omega Institute for Holistic Studies (Rhinebeck, New York) or Canyon Ranch (Tucson, Arizona and Lenox, Massachusetts) Even though it might be with a group of people that have never met you before, their first impressions of you can be invaluable. Ultimately, if there is some sort of disconnect between the way you perceive yourself and the way others perceive you, the signals you give off may not match your inner reality. If there is interference with how clearly you are being seen or heard, then knowing is half the battle.

Even if you disagree, there can be tremendous value in this information. For example, you get feedback that you come across in social situations as distant because your face looks blank and expressionless. You can argue and explain that isn't your intention. You could spend a tremendous amount of time and energy working to change their mind, or you can choose to accept that this is someone else's perception of you and there is an invitation to pay more attention to what you are putting out into the world. Maybe the next time you meet someone new, you'll bring a little extra consciousness to what your face is doing. Perhaps you smile more, or flirt on purpose to give a clearer message that you are interested. It could be that all you need is to hit the gym or a yoga class before going out so that you can be more present with the people around you.

CONSIDER THE SOURCE

Just as important as contemplating the feedback you receive is to consider the source of the feedback. You have to put the feedback you receive into the proper perspective. Some of us are sensitive creatures and one thoughtless word might send us into a tailspin. For example, you might be talking to someone who is projecting all over you. They may give you feedback that you are angry, bitter and hate the world, and perhaps what you are picking up on is their own view of the world filtering in and affecting the way they perceive you. It's also possible that someone has listened to snippets of what you've said and made assumptions about the rest. In this case, you're getting partial feedback and the rest doesn't belong to you. It might be important to take one part of the feedback and leave the rest.

Whatever the case, it's not only important to gather information and feedback, but to challenge it a little bit. Just listen without arguing or defending. Later, you can test the information to see if it's actually true, or make a decision to communicate differently.

The true goal is to be seen as you really are, with a deeper layer of authenticity; not just the surface, but for your deepest self. I think the feedback we get from the universe is how we can tell if things are working—the proof is in the pudding.

WHAT IS THE SOURCE OF YOUR PROBLEMS? TO FIND OUT, START WITH THE MAN IN THE MIRROR.

Once you consider the sources of your feedback, it can be easy to point the finger of your problems outside of yourself. You can look at your bank accounts, your relationships and all of your accomplishments and decide that things happen in life and there is nothing you can do about them. However, this simply isn't true. We are the guardians of our own experience of the world. Our interpretation makes the world a safe place or a scary place; a place filled with possibilities or a place where we are powerless; Heaven or Hell. It depends on the filter you look at the world through.

Let's start with yourself before you weigh opinions from the outside world. An old maxim says that when you point a finger at someone else, you're pointing several fingers back at yourself. A Buddhist principle states that when you are observing something about another person (positive or negative), you are on some level talking about yourself. So if it all starts with ourselves, then we must be able to change our experience of the world (and therefore what we draw to ourselves) by changing our perspective.

Our sense of self is made up of the story we tell ourselves about ourselves. Another name for this is our ego. Contrary to popular belief that the ego is a horrible thing that must be stopped, on some levels, it is vital to our survival. The ego is the sum total of all of our experiences. It helps us to avoid putting our hand on a hot stove and also allows us to state our preferences. The ego is the filter through which we look at the world, and it assigns everything we experience a label so that our brains know where to store the file for later use.

There is a point at which the ego stops being helpful. That point is when it makes us afraid of doing something outside of our past experiences for fear that the unknown might be unpleasant. One way to look at this protective mechanism is to think of a suit of armor. This suit of armor is designed to protect us from harm. It was created by our childhood self, starting with the first time we felt extreme emotion. On that day, a pact was made between our little self and the suit of armor: *Never let me feel something this bad again.* The suit of armor does its job, protecting us from unknown harm. And, like The Terminator did for young John

Connor, it only backs down from a direct command.

Some people say that they hear voices in their head. Some might call them the voice of reason, an angel (or devil) on your shoulder, or whispers of intuition. The voice within us that warns us can be vital to our survival during an emergency (a time where our fight-or-flight response is triggered.) But what do we do with this worry voice when we are in a time of peace? If we are too busy listening to the voice of concern and worry, could we be missing out on another voice?

I have a friend that is an Agape-trained minister, Chemin Bernard. (Agape International Spiritual Center is a science of mind church in Los Angeles created by Reverend Michael Beckwith.) My fiancé and I went to see Chemin before our wedding. I shared with her some old recurring thoughts I had about relationships—worries about trusting another person, and feeling like I had to do everything myself (I could never trust another person as much as I could trust myself). She asked me a pointed and powerful question, which was: Do you want to reassign those voices (that you have used since childhood to protect yourself) now that you're an adult? Give them a new job?" I thought to myself, "I can do that?" I wasn't made wrong for having these voices in my head, and I discovered with Chemin's help that I could direct the energy in a new way.

In the same way, you can too. The next time you're feeling triggered, scared, anxious or worried, try to give that voice a different assignment; something else to focus on. Think about your hot buttons or old patterns of thinking and see if you can direct the part of your brain that's been protecting you to have a new task. Think of it as redirecting a river.

YOUR INNER RADIO

Have you ever woken up in the morning and had a song stuck in your head? Some days are like that. We have a soundtrack that is playing in the background of our daily lives. Some people call this our inner radio station. This radio station can be playing

The way our brain works

According to Freud's structural model of our psyche, there are three parts to our mind: The Id, The Ego and The Superego. To oversimplify these areas for a moment, the Id relates to the pleasure principle, or the short-term desires we seek to have fulfilled. This is a very emotional and intuitive part of our brain. The Ego is the practical, realistic part of us that urges us to be responsible. The Superego is the part of us that determines right from wrong.

Another model (called the Triune brain) refers to three areas of the brain that have developed over time. The three parts are known as the Reptilian Brain, The Limbic System and the NeoCortex. To oversimplify, of these, the Reptilian Brain is the part that represents survival, fight-or-flight mechanisms and worry. The Limbic system deals with motivation and emotion. The NeoCortex allows us to choose our perception of the world. Some people even believe that the NeoCortex is what allows us to perceive an energy or power greater than ourselves.

music, or it might be a talk radio station. There might be a few words stuck on repeat, or a running commentary on the day's events. It might be filled with worries, hopes or dreams. It might be a cheerleader or it might be a critic. Just like an actual radio, you have to tune in to hear what is playing. When you look at the man in the mirror, listen to what your inner radio station is really broadcasting to the world.

You may notice that when you first turn on a water faucet, some orange water comes out of the tap. Once you wait a few seconds, the water clears as the new water flushes out the rust from the pipes it is being carried through. Sometimes it's like that with our minds. You may settle down to rest at night and find that your mind is going a million miles an hour. Consider using a notebook or journal to write out some of the thoughts racing through your head. Sometimes by putting these thoughts down on paper, the "orange water" from your inner radio station is flushed out and your mind can once again flow clearly. As you change the relationship with your inner radio (like changing the dial to a new and better station), you start to ask yourself different questions.

BETTER OUT THAN IN

The Artists Way is a beautiful book written by Julia Cameron. It contains dozens of tips, exercises and nuggets of wisdom for those seekers who are looking for a process to explore internally. One of the things I highly recommend reading is her section on morning pages and evening pages. She recommends writing until you fill up three pages first thing in the morning and right before bed. You might write out your dreams, worries, a laundry list or simply "I don't know what to write" until you fill the pages. It's a great way of getting what is stuck in your head out and onto paper, which can increase creativity by allowing us to be a clear channel for what wants to come through.

Years ago, I created an evening ritual for myself where I wrote out my schedule for the next day and wrote any remaining thoughts about my day into a journal. This process was my version of evening pages. After I was finished, my mind could relax and my sleep was deeper and more restful than it had been. To this day, I spend a few minutes before bed reviewing my day and focusing on the next day's tasks, and that gives me an opportunity to take some of the information I might have been storing away and put it someplace. First thing in the morning, after I've emerged from the bedroom, the first thing I do is look down at that list and get some perspective on what my day holds for me. Just that process alone has been life changing.

The next time you find your mind racing when it's time for bed,

A three-step process for making decisions

Once you become aware of what's playing on your inner radio station, you have to make a decision about whether or not to do anything about it. To make a decision about something, here's the process I always take my clients through: gather, weigh, decide. You'll see this as a recurring theme throughout the book.

Making a decision always starts with self-discovery. Before we can make a decision, we have to gather information. If we don't do that crucial step first, we may use partial information and guess the rest, which leads to decisions fraught with tension and anxiety. Instead, try using this three-step process when you need to make a choice about something. (Remember this process, which will be mentioned in later chapters of this book.)

1] Gather information
2] Weigh your options
3] Make your decision

We can liken these steps to the advice earlier in this chapter. The first step is to gather information about a situation; this is the gathering of feedback. Until you have all the information, you are most likely going to make some assumptions that could cloud the picture, your decision and the results.

The second step is to weigh your options about the situation; considering the source of the feedback you gathered. During this process you might compare and contrast one option against the others. You could create a pro/con list. This will help you gain clarity when making your decision.

The third step is to make your decision—deciding what you want to change about what you put out into the world. Whether you are the type of person who thinks things through carefully, makes the decision from your gut, or feels what your heart has to say, the important thing is to make the decision, then trust the answer you come up with.

consider trying this process. You may wish to release whatever is mentally and spiritually weighing on you. You may process core beliefs about yourself that you don't want to identify anymore. Regardless of the subject you focus on, this practice can help you create an inner lightness as you drift off to sleep.

A MENTAL VACATION

If you're experiencing repetitive mental chatter and need a break, it can sometimes feel like you need a vacation from your own mind. The problem seems to be that wherever you go, there you are. So how can you create a mini-mental vacation for yourself? There are ways to work outside in, which means changing something in your external environment that may help give you a break from your nonstop thoughts.

In a world where we are often sedentary—working at a desk, sitting in front of a screen or riding in cars, buses and planes—it can be important to get the energy moving somewhere besides our brains for a little while. Go for a run, dance, make love… do something physical so that you're not just living life from the neck up. Sometimes we might feel as though our brains are getting overheated like a car engine or a computer. In this case, the best thing might be to sit in quiet, get a massage or take a bath; anything to help us slow down our racing thoughts and decompress.

Another way to take a mental vacation might be to change what you put inside your body. See if you can cut out foods and beverages that create high highs and low lows. Too much sugar, caffeine or heavy spices may create a system that is out of balance. At the same time, add in foods that are simple, alive and filled with minerals and nutrients. This can change things in a hurry.

If you're still experiencing unwanted chatter inside your head, here's a great way to change what you are focusing on immediately. Just as if you

> "Mental imprints are planted in the mind through the gates of our own awareness of ourselves as we do anything to help or hurt another. The strength with which they are planted depends on various factors, including our intentions, the strength of our emotions, how well we recognize what we're doing, etc. The camera of our mind records about 65 discreet images or imprints during the space of a single finger snap. These imprints enter a place in our subconscious. Here they remain for days or years or decades, reproducing themselves every millisecond like frames of a movie. Seeds within the stream of the mind continue to grow after they have been planted in an exponential way. The magnitude of a mental imprint planted on the first of the month has doubled by the second, is quadrupled by the third and by the fifth of the month is 16 times its original strength. Consider the weight of a single acorn as opposed to the weight of the resulting oak tree...mental seeds behave no differently. "

—Geshe Michael Roach
excerpted from The Diamond Cutter

were watching a scary movie that you didn't like, you could just change the channel; in this same way, you can also change the channel in your mind. One of my teachers shared a way to do this whenever thoughts popped into my mind that I didn't want to be there. Let's say a paranoid thought creeps in and you don't like how it makes you feel. Say the words *"cancel, cancel"* out loud and it can help you change your focus to something new. I do this when I picture something bad happening. Sometimes it feels automatic.

For example, at the beginning of my most recent relationship, I realized that both of us were having these sudden moments of panic while we were falling in love. Those thoughts were "What if something happens to you?" It was because we cared so much that on some level, an old part of us worried that we may lose it, but because we didn't want to focus on that, we started to use "cancel, cancel" to change the channel and refocus on something good.

Sometimes people are able to stop thinking about a certain subject, but unless they change their thoughts to a new subject, the old thought creeps back in again. Remember, nature abhors a vacuum, so if you eliminate something, put something new in its place. Picture something that makes you feel good—a person you love, a pet or a beautiful piece of art that uplifts you when you see it. Perhaps you put on some of your favorite music. Shift your focus to something positive and beautiful. It may not be just one thing that gets you there, but a combination of things. Any or all of it can help.

THE POWER IS IN THE QUESTION: STARTING THE PROCESS OF SHIFTING

In this process of self-discovery, you might find that there are things other people think about you, or that you think about yourself, that you don't like very much. For example, you might hear that you are lazy, or hypercritical of yourself or others. You may learn that the first voice that you hear in your head is negative. Once you notice something about yourself, you may realize you're thinking it more and more often. Pretty soon you are saying it to other people, and the cycle continues. Now it's part of your identity and part of how you are seen in the world. But what does all this mean? "Lazy. Critical. Negative." Does this mean that it's *always* true?

For example, it may feel as though you are "always" negative. It may not be true, but you may believe that it is. Consider asking yourself *Is it true that I am always negative?* If you stop to question it, you may find that at least one time in the history of your life, you weren't negative. Now you cannot say that you are always negative. This isn't just semantics. It opens up a way of looking at yourself in which something new can happen. You are not a finished product. You are not a noun, but a verb. You continue to be a new person, each day, each moment, and in these moments you can choose anew. Then it begs the question *Are you the adjective you say you are?* Or are you just *being that* in some moments?

I have a life coaching client who showed up at a workshop where I brought up this concept of a story that we tell ourselves about ourselves. The example she gave is "I'm always late." As soon as I heard the word always, it made me wonder, is it actually true? I asked if there was ever a time that she could recall that she was on time; even once? Her face changed and her body language softened and she said, "I'm sure there are a few times that I've been on time, but it's not the usual." I said to the

---

The Work by Byron Katie

Byron Katie is a powerful author who utilizes a series of questions designed to challenge the way we look at ourselves and break through the blocks that may be keeping us from seeing ourselves clearly. She has created a series of four questions called "The Work" that helps people access their authentic selves by breaking down old core beliefs. By the power contained within these four questions, she has helped many people change their lives. **For the four questions, support materials and additional information, go to thework.com.**

---

group, "Can you see the difference between saying 'I am always this...' versus 'My tendency has been to do this...' " It sometimes helps us to feel like it's not our fate to always be late, it's more of a bad habit. The change in wording creates some space around it to do something about it and change the story you're telling yourself.

The questions you ask yourself are more powerful than the answers you decide about yourself. For example, you can ask *why* an infinite amount of times. Spend some time with friends under the age of 10 and you might be invited to play a game with no end. Why, why? WHY?! Questions have power because they can activate our curiosity. It's rarely as fulfilling to get the answer as it is to ask the question. The power therefore lies in the asking of the question, not in the actual answer.

You can also use questions to reframe something you are curious about. Let's say you ask yourself *Can I stop being so negative?* There is a

50-50 chance of success. The answer to this question will be either "Yes, I can," or "No, I can't." There is a possibility that you may fail. (Side note: You might say to yourself that you don't know the answer. This may be honest, but it isn't very empowering.) Now what happens if you add the word *how* to the front of the question? "*How* can I stop being so negative?" This question activates your curiosity around the possibility of success. Now your mind is working on possibilities of steps you can take which may lead you to find a solution to how you can stop being so negative. There are many types of questions you can ask, and all of them can lead you to a deeper awareness of yourself and what is possible.

ONE STEP AT A TIME

Every once in a while, we need to overhaul our self-image. We may notice that after many years of judgment and criticism that our confidence is at an all-time low. Imagine that we move through life on an ocean of consciousness. Our sense of ourselves might be the boat we use to move

Tell the truth

Try an experiment with the truth if only for a few minutes, a few hours or a few days. See if you can commit to telling the truth in every situation possible. Test the waters by telling yourself the truth of how you actually feel. As you tell yourself the truth, it may give you the confidence to be truthful with others. Telling people the truth is coming from a place of authenticity instead of trying to say what you think people want to hear. If you're worried about how your words will be received, you can take extra care to deliver your message with sweetness. It might soften the blow, especially if your words are unexpected. Even if people are initially stung by what you say, your opinion will be incredibly valuable because people will know that if they ask you a question, you will tell them the truth. People will trust you more and you will trust yourself more.

through our lives. Over time, our boats can grow leaks which slow us down, force us to bail water, or abandon our means of transportation altogether.

They say that Rome wasn't built in a day. Neither is our self-esteem. If you find that you are rebuilding the image of yourself, be patient. Acknowledge the little victories. It may be two steps forward and two steps back for a while, but it is always done one step at a time. If you get impatient at your growth or do things too fast, it makes for sloppy work. You are building the foundation of the image of yourself—this is not something that needs to be rushed. Keep things simple, slow down and put one foot in front of the other to set yourself up for success.

One of the ways that you can build confidence in yourself is to tell the truth as often as possible. If you are someone who tells the truth, and you know that you tell the truth, then your confidence will go up because you recognize that you are a person with strong integrity. The added benefit is that when you make a statement about your future, those words are going to have more power to them, because you are a person who tells the truth! So whether you are commenting on something that already exists or making a prediction, the world won't be able to distinguish the two and your ability to manifest what you say you want to do will increase. Practically speaking, whatever you are thinking about sets into motion your words, deeds and action. In time, this becomes our destiny.

In his book *The Four Agreements*, author Don Miguel Ruiz suggests that we be impeccable with our word. One aspect of that is to tell the truth. If you only tell the truth some of the time, you won't trust yourself because if you can lie to others, you might be lying to yourself on some level. It can be very important and empowering to consistently tell yourself the truth.

YODA WAS RIGHT

Another way to build confidence is to do what you say you are going to do. This is a cornerstone of integrity, and integrity builds confidence. It's also another way of telling the truth. One of the ways we let ourselves off the hook is by using the word "try." We might set out to do something with the best of intentions, but something derails us. If someone confronts us, we can always say, "I tried."

But what does this actually mean? Does it mean that you partially did something? This isn't possible. You're either writing the book you say you want to write, or you're not. You may have stopped doing something before you accomplished your goal, but that means you aren't doing it. Trying is nothing more than an excuse, and ultimately it doesn't make you or the person you are speaking to feel any better. As the wise Yoda once said, "Do or do not. There is no try."

RELEASE AND LET GO

At the end of the day, nothing will make you feel better about a situation than doing your best. Your best may change from moment to moment, as what you can give in this moment may be only 20% of what you are capable of after a nourishing meal or a good night's rest. But if you are doing your best, you will never regret it or wish for a do-over, and this will make it

Create a sacred fire

Here's a way to release parts of your story that are no longer serving you. Get some recycled paper (or perhaps some Joss paper made from bamboo or rice) and tear it into strips. On each strip of paper, write down a negative thing you are convinced is true about yourself (preferably with non-toxic ink). Read them one at a time, then place them into a biodegradable bag. Once you have gone through each of the pieces of paper or the bag is full, close it and hold it in your hands. Say thank you for all of the things you are aware of about yourself, then place the bag into a fire. (If you don't have access to a fire, you can bury the bag underground, place it into the ocean, or imagine the fire in your mind and shred the papers and put them into the trash.) If you are ready to release part of the old negative story about yourself, this is a way of making space for grace to enter.

easier to accept that whatever happens is actually for your highest good.

After doing your best, you can't do any more, so there is no reason to second-guess or worry. As the Dalai Lama says in the *Art of Happiness*, "If there is anything you can do about a situation… anything at all… then do it, but don't worry about it. And if there is nothing you can do about a situation, then don't worry about it…because there is nothing you can do!" In both situations, he takes away the opportunity for us to worry. This also happens when we do our best; it quiets the part of the brain that likes to worry.

Sometimes after doing all of the work, the only thing left to do is to let go and trust the process. Let's say you want to grow some plants. First, you get a plot of land. Then you clear the garbage, weeds and rocks from the soil. Next you plant some seeds, water the land and stand back. You might want to protect the land from invaders, keep it watered and pull up the occasional weeds; these are things you can do. You wouldn't want to dig up the seeds at night to see if they are growing; it wouldn't help the situation. Neither will worrying about it.

Career and Service

"If you have to support yourself, you had bloody well better find some way that is going to be interesting." —Katherine Hepburn

YOUR PATH OF SERVICE: DEFINING WHAT YOU DO

Many of us are defined by what we do. In fact, most of the time, when people meet for the first time, they ask each other what the other person does within the first few minutes of the conversation. It can tell us a lot about a person: what they are skilled at, what their interests are and sometimes whether they are making money.

What it doesn't tell us is if the person is happy. It doesn't tell us whether or not the person is expressing their gifts and talents in a

> ### Feng Shui principle: Aloha
>
> Aloha refers to many different things to the people of Hawaii. It is generally recognized as a greeting filled with love and respect. It can also mean the breath of life and the sending and receiving of positive energy. If you have ever been to Hawaii, you can recognize when people are doing something with the spirit of Aloha. It's very palpable.

Color your world

The best colors for career and service are colors that relate with the mysteries of the unknown and with the elements water and metal. Rich blacks and dark blues represent the deep flowing water. Clean whites, metallic grays and sea foam greens are also helpful.

meaningful way, or doing something good for the world.

My friend and meditation teacher Julie Zipper likes to say "You are not your job. It is not the source of your happiness. Neither is your bank account and neither is your relationship. It's something else." Your source of happiness is something else; your career is your career.

A job or career might be defined as the work you do on a regular basis to pay your bills. The way most people think of their job is that it is something they must do. They see it as an obligation; a duty. It isn't necessarily synonymous with happiness or your dream job. It is simply what you offer the world in exchange for compensation.

There are some people who are living their dream. They may or may not be well compensated for it, but they are getting up every day and doing what they love to do. It might be a hobby, taking care of other people or even volunteering. There are a fortunate few who are extremely well paid to do what they love to do. Perhaps one of the first questions we should be asking isn't "What do you do?" but rather "How do you feel about what you do?"

Ultimately, our path of fulfillment is found in doing what we say we want to do. If you say you just want to make money because that's what's most important to you, then do that. If you say that you want to be creatively fulfilled, do that. But as we mentioned in an earlier chapter, we don't want to create win-lose scenarios. If you feel that you might be committing to one of these things at the expense of something else, then you might be out of balance.

START QUESTIONING

If you are miserable in your job, you may want to start by expanding your definition of what it means to have a job. In feng shui, this is the equivalent of making some space. By asking a few simple questions, we may start to open up new possibilities in our thoughts. Instead of thinking about the logistics of what is available and how much you will be paid, start exploring some of the principles such as:

- Do you like being around people?
- Or do you prefer to work alone?
- Do you like being creative at work?
- Or would you rather put things in order?
- Do you wish you could travel more? Less?
- Would you prefer to work outdoors?
- Or do you like working at a desk?

I did this questioning exercise with a client of mine who worked in finance who, for years, had consistently worked as a CFO of large corporations. He was miserable, and he kept finding himself in similar situations. A recurring theme was that he kept having the same boss in different bodies. Inevitably, the boss would say things that cut my client's confidence down, which reinforced the fact that he didn't feel like enough. My client, who was paid a handsome salary and lived in a very nice area, had a wife and child to provide for and, thinking of college tuition, started to feel trapped. He felt like there was nothing he could to do get out of the job because of his obligations, so he said he felt like he had to suck it up and stay.

We had some conversations about what else he'd like to do, and he kept saying he was stumped on that because he never had the time to think about it. One day he called and said he was being laid off with a handsome severance, and now he was going to have plenty of time to think about what he wanted to do next. We started to think outside the box and explored different areas that had interested him at previous times in his life. Through the series of questions, he didn't necessarily identify the job that he truly wanted to do, but he knew the qualities that his ideal job entailed. He started to feel more empowered, because whether it was a job that was offered to him or that he created himself, he now knew what was important to him in what he was looking for. A few months later, he did get a new job offer in the same field and after much consideration, decided to take it. Even though it was in a similar field, he's now in a completely different—and more importantly, better—relationship with his boss and his work.

PURPOSE

It has been said, "If you always do what you always did, you'll always get what you always got." Some of us are suffering because we don't feel as though we have any options. We feel trapped by the way things are and powerless to make things the way we'd like them to be. We might plod along for a while accepting our fate. But if our point of dissatisfaction gets strong enough, we may finally gain the courage to change. It has to start with recognition that things cannot remain the way they are any longer.

One of the things that can help us break the cycle of the way things are is to elevate our career to something with deeper meaning. According to the Bhagavad Gita, the path of yoga called Karma Yoga is about being of service to the world. The idea behind it is that if we do things with a higher purpose in mind, then we will feel closer to the divine. Instantly, the shift moves away from *what am I getting from my job?* to *what am I bringing to it?*

My Zen Teacher and dear friend Yasuhiko Kimura used to encourage us to distinguish our job from our J.O.B., which stands for Joy Of Being. He encouraged us to get in touch with that which we came here to do. Whether we look at this as what we were meant to do, our highest calling or our reason for being, each of these aligns with a deeper sense of purpose. Once I discovered what mine was, I finally started to understand what people meant when they said "Do what you love and you'll never work a day in your life."

One way to discover if you're living your purpose is to ask yourself if your job expresses your joy. According to Leo Buscaglia, "Ancient Egyptians believed that, upon death, they would be asked two questions and their answers would determine whether they could continue their journey in the afterlife. The first question was, 'Did you bring joy?' The second was, 'Did you find joy?'" If our jobs are not bringing joy to ourselves or others, we may want to rethink our commitments to what we are doing.

GUT CHECK TIME: SOMETHING NEEDS TO CHANGE

I had a client couple that had experienced a tremendous amount of success prior to moving to Los Angeles. When they arrived, they faced an integration process where they were forced to challenge what they were doing and the way they were doing it. When they called me, we started to dig a little bit to determine what might energetically be keeping them stagnant. It turned out that the husband and wife had different visions of where they wanted to live. One, deep down, wanted to live in New York City, and the other really wanted to be in Los Angeles; something obviously needed to shift for them to continue as a couple.

I talked to them about the concept of two or more people being gathered in the name of something, and that within their relationship, to be aligned was much more powerful than being pulled in different directions. We discussed a vision that allowed for both of their needs to get met, which included splitting time in both places through vacations and creating a dream home in New York (a pied-a-terre) sometime in the future. That freed up their energy and allowed them to focus on where they were in the moment. From then on, they were a team again and all sorts of paths started opening up on their journey.

If you have now realized without a doubt that something needs to change in your life, the next step is in determining what to change first. It might seem obvious, but there are really only three categories of choices:

1. Change what you are doing.
2. Change your approach to what you are doing.

3. Keep doing the same thing and waiting for something outside of you to change your circumstances.

You can work toward your goal in one of two ways: outside in, or inside out. Outside in means changing something outside of you that will bring about a change inside. Inside out means changing something inside you that will in turn affect your outer circumstances. Lasting change tends to occur when we do a little bit of both, but for the purposes of exploration, let's take them one step at a time.

STEP 1
Kicking it up a notch: Change your value
EXPLORE AN INCREASE IN YOUR SALARY

Most of the time, our frustration comes from not having enough money. People often complain that they are not paid enough to do what they are doing. Start asking yourself if your financial picture changed, would that change how you are feeling about what you are doing? How will you know if this is true? Start by imagining it. If you added a few hundred dollars a week to your salary, would that make the job feel any better? Sure, we would all like to add a few zeros to our salary, but start small and work your way up from there. Keep increasing the amount until you notice your feelings about the job shift in a more positive direction. You may have discovered the key to making this job work, for now.

I had one client who was suffering because she was doing a support job in order to do what she really wanted to do. She really wanted to leave the support job, so she came up with the courage to ask for an increase in her salary and was determined that if she didn't get it, she would find something new. Once she asked for the increase at the support job, she got it. Getting the raise changed her relationship with the support job, and she ended up being okay with staying. When the frustrating parts of a job outweigh the benefits, that's usually the time to shake things up. This was her way of shaking things up.

STEP 2
Discover the value of your time

One client that taught me the valuable lesson in calculating the value of time was a film editor I was thinking of hiring for a movie I had directed. The film editor was a person who had had tremendous success on the East Coast and was now in L.A. This person was having a hard time balancing excitement about my project and a minimum dollar amount he would feel comfortable with. When I asked him what it was, he said it's the amount of money I can accept and not be looking at the clock all day, wondering when the project would be over. He knew exactly what that number was, and it wasn't the most money he had ever made. That stood out to me as a great example of someone who knew the value of his time.

You may receive a change in your salary simply by envisioning it. It sometimes happens, but not always. More than likely, you'll need to speak up and ask for what you want. Before committing to that conversation, the first step is to feel you deserve what you are asking for.

On top of the world

It was once calculated that an hour of Michael Jordan's time at the peak of his career was worth something like $15,000. People joked that if he went to the movies, he could "make $30,000 just by sitting there." Not a bad salary for someone who knew he had tremendous value.

Start by figuring out the value of your time. Do you know what an hour of your time is worth? Lawyers know how much they bill to companies who hire them. If you can figure out what an hour of your time is worth, then you can decide if it is worth it to you to do whatever you are committed to doing. Whether you use this value to measure against an hour at your job, an hour helping someone else, or an hour watching football, it can help put things into perspective for you.

I've had clients who were afraid to speak up (due to the economy, some worry or fear or some external authority figure telling them not to rock the boat). Some of those people stayed in uncomfortable situations for years, but the moment of change finally came from giving themselves permission and taking courage to ask for what they wanted. Once they knew the value of their time, they were able to speak up. They also knew that if they heard "No," it was okay. Some left their situations and some stayed, but all were led closer to their heart. They were more empowered to speak their truth regardless of the outcome.

STEP 3
How to figure out the value of an hour of your time

The following examples are a few different ways of determining the value of your time.

1. Divide your current salary by the number of hours you work. Example: If your salary is $500 a week and you work 40 hours a week, each hour would be valued at $12.50. This can be helpful as a starting reference point.

2. Find out what the market will bear and what other people are being paid for similar work. There can be incredible value in doing research. Even if the news that comes back isn't pleasant, it can be useful as a measuring stick to help you determine what your worth is.

3. Create a budget of what your life costs each week and divide that amount by the amount of hours you work. Example: Let's say your life costs you $750 a week and you work 40 hours. At this rate, each hour is worth $18.75. (Note: Since you are basing this off of the amount your life costs, you need to factor in that this is the amount you need to earn per hour after taxes and other deductions.)

4. Create an ideal budget of what your life costs and divide that amount by all the hours you work each month. This could be inclusive of your primary job, the job you are working at but aren't getting paid for yet, the time you volunteer and help other people, and the time that you do your training or go to school to prepare for a future job. Now divide the total hours by your ideal budget. Example: If your ideal budget is $5,000 a week and you are working a total of 80 hours per week toward your dreams, then your time is worth $62.50. If your current salary is not allowing you to afford some of the things in your life that you have determined are important, then this can be the motivation you need to make a change.

So what have you started to notice? You might find that you're getting $35 an hour, but you need $50 an hour if you want to start saving for something big—a house, a car, your wedding, etc. The message is clear: your choice is to find more hours you can work, or work the same amount and charge more.

People may not offer you more money unless you tell them what you want. This may entail setting a boundary in your mind and then standing up for it. The conversation may go seamlessly, or it may be a difficult one, but the results will give you information on whether you stay in this job, ask for something else which will help you feel valued (such as additional vacation time or perhaps a work-at-home day each week), or give you the courage to look elsewhere.

STEP 4
Ask for what you want

If you don't ask, you will never know if you can get it. The answer
that comes back may not be what you want to hear, but you want to do
whatever you can to set yourself up for success. Three things to
consider are that in any request, there is a time, a way and a place to ask
for what you want.

TIMING

We can have a harder time feeling empowered when we are tired, hungry
or overwhelmed. Make sure you get some good rest, work out if you can
and put some healthy, nourishing food in your belly. If the timing doesn't
feel right, you can always push it back. Remember, you may never feel
100% ready, and at a certain point you will just have to leap off the cliff.

Also consider the timing for the other person. You may not want to ask
for something for you (win) while the other person is feeling
grumpy (lose.) It may not be best to set the meeting for first thing in the
morning (when people are just waking up), just before lunch (when they
might be hungry), just after lunch (when they might be in a food coma),
or at the end of the day (when they might be tired, hungry and
overwhelmed by trying to get home.) Based on the person's schedule and
personality, try to choose a time that he or she would be most open to
this type of conversation.

THE WAY

As you prepare for your meeting, get yourself into a place where you feel strong, positive and ready for whatever comes. If you need to, chat with a friend, coach or family member to remind you of what is important. If you can't find another person, listen to an iPod with your favorite tunes or to an inspirational recording, such as Wayne Dyer's *Excuses Begone*. Do what you need to do to remember your dreams and your value.

During the conversation, state what you want cleanly, simply and directly. Don't be vague. Don't apologize. Look the other person in the eye and really see the human being in there. They say you can attract more flies with honey than with vinegar. Work to bring some of the aloha spirit into the conversation.

THE PLACE

It can feel overwhelming to go into someone else's space to ask for what you need. Energetically, it can give the other person a psychological and even an energetic advantage to have this conversation in their space. Ideally, pick a space that levels the playing field a bit, or, if you can have it in your own office, it may even give you the edge. At the very least, choose a neutral space like a conference room, coffee shop or restaurant. Most of the time we don't get a choice, but given an option, see if you can set yourself up for success by picking a place that energetically suits you.

If you cannot pick the location, see if you can sit in a place that makes you feel more empowered. If you consider the metaphor of something "having your back," try to sit with something behind you. You may not be able to get a couple of bodyguards, but a wall, a plant or even a piece of art work is better than leaving your "back" vulnerable. Regardless of any external circumstances, there is one place that can always be within your realm of control: your mind.

STEP 5
One level deeper: Change your mind

Congratulations! You've asked for a raise. Whether you hear the answer you want to hear or one that you don't, there is an invitation here to prepare for a deeper level of change. Let's say you receive the raise. Does this mean you will be happier? If so, why not start now, preparing for a future that is brighter and feels better to you? If you don't receive the raise and you have done everything you can, you may be faced with a choice to stay at the job or not to stay. But before you come to that decision, there is another place to explore: your attitude and your thoughts.

I had one client list a series of reasons why she couldn't make a change in her life. At a certain point, it became comical because she was actually manufacturing reasons that didn't exist, and I told her so. I playfully referred to her as an excuse factory. It was tough for her to hear, but she got it. It was a turning point to her to address her underlying concern of not having enough, which really came from a worry of not being enough. By addressing this underlying thought pattern, she learned to patch her leaky boat and once again set sail.

POVERTY CONSCIOUSNESS

Some people expect to fail. On some level, they feel as though they are powerless to influence their lives and when news comes back, it is most likely going to be unfavorable. Whether you call this realistic, pessimistic or a glass-half empty mentality, there is an identification with some degree of failure going on. It is possible that under the surface this person doesn't feel deserving of receiving what they say they want.

Energy vampires

Sometimes the things that are draining us are the people we have in our closest circle. I have heard of these people referred to as "energy vampires" because they leave us feeling drained after we spend time with them in person or talking on the phone. There are many ways that people can steal our energy. They may be convinced that they are victims all the time. Sometimes you have had to listen to endless chatter for hours at a time. You may hear them complain, gossip or spout negativity toward the world. Other forms of energy stealing include fishing for compliments, asking for endless advice (sometimes the very same advice you have given time and time again) or offering unsolicited opinions about your own life. It's possible that these conversations or actions are being done unconsciously, but if you are feeling repeatedly drained after spending time with certain people, it may be important to start thinking about what you both get from the relationship.

Maybe you feel guilty letting them go, or you don't know whom else they might turn to. You might want to remember the concept of win-win. Our resources are precious. Our time, our attention, our energy are all gifts that we can share with others. When you share these gifts, do you feel as though they are being received? Or do you feel as though they are, to some degree, going to waste? Sometimes it is a matter of changing the subject. Other times, it may be calling attention to the imbalance and setting a clear boundary within the relationship. In extreme cases, you may need to walk away altogether. It all depends on your priorities. Being drained leaves you no good to yourself or anyone around you.

I have done this. I've taken space from dating people, friendships, jobs and even family members that felt like they were draining me. Simply by taking space from those situations, I felt an immediate impact on my overall energy levels and my ability to stay positive. The closer we are to someone, the harder it is, but it's very important. Sometimes we need to find a way to transform the relationship because we can't take space from it. No matter who it is or how important it is, remember that this is an option. You can always revisit the relationship down the road.

When you pay attention to people's language an interesting thing happens. Sometimes patterns emerge. Listen to people's excuses: "I'm so busy," "I'm broke," "I'm exhausted," "I'm alone and I have too much to do." All of these imply some sort of lack. In order: time, money, energy and help. If you feel as though you don't have enough, it is possible that underneath it all you don't feel like enough. Perhaps your inner thoughts are having outward effects. It's like trying to sail a leaky boat. No matter how fast you try to go, there is something underneath slowing you down, draining you, asking for your attention, asking to be fixed. Why not plug the hole once and for all? Identify what you believe to be lacking and shine the light of your attention on it to take the first step toward healing once and for all.

STEP 6
Be grateful

Reclaiming your energy is a great start toward changing your experience and your circumstances, but if you really want to get things moving, there's nothing quite like applying the principle of gratitude. When we focus on all the things we don't have, things we are irritated by and things that make us feel drained, it can help us identify things we want to work on. If all we do is focus on those things, we may find ourselves in an endless loop, attracting and re-attracting the same situations with different faces and names. One of the ways to shift the focus is to appreciate what you *do* have.

This can be easier said than done. The suggestion is to start with the obvious (things in your life that make you feel good—this could be your lover, the sunshine on your face or getting a massage). It's easy to be grateful for the things that make us feel good.

It is slightly more difficult to be grateful for things that are neutral, stuff we can take or leave; that which makes us say "meh." If you can apply the principle of gratitude to these neutral items, it may change your perception of the world. Neutral items include things you may take for granted such as your health, the air you breathe and having a roof above your head every night. In addition, these items help us draw a contrast between you and those who don't have as much. In the process, it will increase our experience of gratitude in our lives.

The hardest items to be grateful for are things we dislike, that annoy us, or that we hate. However, if we have started building momentum with the things that make us feel good and then items that are neutral, it may eventually be possible to experience gratitude toward things that start out appearing bloody awful. These could include obligations, things that startle us or things that initially appear negative. Focusing on what you're irritated about may just motivate you to quit. Psychiatrist Carl Jung is known for saying, "What you resist, persists." If you keep focusing on negatives, you'll get more of them. There is another way.

One of my first jobs in Los Angeles was being a messenger who delivered packages to movie studios. It started out as something unpleasant, then downgraded to something I despised. My chiropractor suggested a challenge. She suggested that I work at being grateful for my job. She told me that if I was grateful every day for this job, I wouldn't have to do it for very long and I would never have to do it again. I thought this was impossible at first. I detested this job. I felt underappreciated, underpaid and my car was taking a beating. I tried what she suggested: practicing gratitude on a daily basis. It wasn't easy, but it was really important to me to change my situation.

Within a month, I was offered a job that required me to travel out of the country for a few months, first in Paris, then in Edinburgh, Scotland, with my closest friends. One night while walking in Edinburgh, I was contemplating my return home and what I would do for work when I got there. I made a personal vow: I will no longer take jobs from a place of fear.

Then suddenly, the whole world changed. Within a week of my return home to Los Angeles, the World Trade Center in New York was attacked, and I couldn't get a job. Even though I had made that vow, I researched all options, but no one was hiring. It was like the universe was guiding me, saying *I got your back.* I decided to give away one session of life coaching to person in need and a feng shui consultation to another, and I have had a word-of-mouth feng shui business ever since. The experience really made me appreciate my inner voice.

The opposite of appreciation is taking things for granted. Check your attitude about the job you're currently in. It's possible you're just frustrated and focusing on all the things you don't like and if you change your attitude, it might change how you feel about the job. People may pick up on your new energy. Even if you don't leave the job, perhaps you may not feel as frazzled or bothered as much by it. If you appreciate the job and the things it brings into your life, you may find yourself being more appreciated by others and then you may get more of what you were hoping for from the job to begin with. At the very least, your experience may become more positive for as long as you still have to be there, or the process may help give you the energy to manifest something else.

STEP 7
Change that job

Sometimes, we are left with no other choice but to change jobs. Either the situation becomes so toxic, so negative or so challenging that the best thing to do is get out and regroup so that we can manifest something new. After you have tried asking for what you deserve and shifting your attitude, it may become clear that the universe has other plans. In feng shui terms, you may have to make some space in order for something new to come into your life.

If you find out you aren't doing what you want to do, the question isn't *if* you're going to quit, it's *when* and *how*. For some people, depending on your circumstances, quitting your job before finding the next one is the best thing because it will give you the motivation you need to change (of course, only do this if it's feasible to you—you have savings to support yourself or someone who can help with living expenses until you find another job). You may find after taking this leap that you have all the courage you need. For other people, having a plan of attack will help avoid creating a panic or sense of being overwhelmed.

STEP 8
Identify your true calling

Imagine that you woke up one day and were doing something you loved so much you could hardly believe that people were willing to pay you to do it. Have you heard stories like this? They do exist. As Mark Twain once said, "Work and play are words used to describe the same thing under different circumstances." In order to step into this new job, you may need to find it or you may need to create it, but first you have to know what you are looking for.

The first step in the process of attracting or creating your dream job is to be clear about what it is. You may need to gather some information first. When people are confronted with the question "What do you really want to do with your life?" they may have any number of reactions. A common one for people who are not used to thinking this way is to say "I don't know."

In my experience, "I don't know" means one of two different things. Either it means that you don't actually have the information (as in, what happened on the 12th day of December in the year 1149 on the island of Fiji?). Or it could mean that you know two things and they are in conflict with each other (I know that I want to be my own boss, and I know that I am scared to be my own boss).

Perhaps you will discover that you want to do something but you don't believe that you can make money doing it. You may need to weed your garden of old thoughts (I'm not worthy of getting paid to do what I love to do) or you may need to do some research (Do I know someone who does what I want to be doing and is getting paid for it?). If you have a career in mind, talk to people in it to gather information and ask to shadow someone in that job to test drive it. As I mentioned in chapter three, the process for making any decision is always the same: Gather information; Weigh your options; Make your decision.

STEP 9
Your job is to find THE job

Yasuhiko would suggest, "Pick the thing you most want to do in the world—something you're willing to live or die for—and charge well for it." This reminds me of the feng shui principle at the beginning of the chapter: the principle of Aloha.

Buddha said "Your work is to discover *your* work, and then with all your heart to give yourself to it." An important place to start gathering information on the job you wish to create may start with volunteering. The way you wish to be of service may have nothing to do with what you eventually get paid for. Perhaps it's a job that you may call a hobby. Other paths of service, such as tutoring, mentoring, playing music, being a parent or something else that doesn't necessarily pay a salary may be the way you prefer to give service. The things that light up your

Our Deepest Passion

My teacher and friend Yasuhiko Kimura has created something called The Passion Workshop, which is designed for us to discover our deepest passion, the reason we came to earth. The course is more about the process of self-discovery rather than learning some secret answer that is being hidden from the world. Within the course, we are asked a series of questions that help us to get a clearer idea of what our deepest passion is. He asks a variation on the following questions:

- If you no longer needed to rest, what would you do with your time?
- If you had unlimited resources at your disposal, what would you do with your time?
- If you had one day to live, what message would you share with the world?
- If everyone were healthy, enlightened and didn't need you to save them, what would you do with your time?
- If time were no longer a factor (if you could never die), what would you do for eternity?

Each of these questions were designed to get us out of the box of our thinking and to hint at a deeper sense of what is most important to us.

heart may attract to you all the information and people you need to make your dreams a reality.

At first when you explore what is out there, you may stay inside the box. You may look to what is safe, and that's fine. But recognize that going down that path may lead to you to another job that has you questioning the very same things down the road. It might have a different name and different faces, but the circumstances are identical. To avoid this, ask yourself questions outside the box. Remember that the power is in the questions you ask. You don't want a job you can tolerate; you want a job that you love, so it's really important to come up with all the qualities that you want that job to have and do the brain dump exercise.

Make a list of all of the qualities you would like to have in a job.

Write down everything you can think of, from most important to least important. Whether it's working with people, having your own office or traveling more, make a list of all the qualities you can think of in the kind of work you'd ideally like to do. Then separate the list into deal breakers (the conditions the job *must* meet for you to enjoy it) and strong preferences. Deal breakers go up top, strong preferences down below. As jobs come along, put them through this process. (This is the same exercise recommended at the end of chapter 2; you can use it to find out if any given person, thing or situation meets your needs.)

As we talked about with relationships, in an ideal situation, all the deal breakers need to be met and strong preferences need to average 80% or more. Take this checklist and hold it up to any job you've ever had or want. Sometimes an item won't be able to be scored because you don't have enough information yet. If so, write down not available (N/A); that means there's more information to be gathered. Gather as much information as you can about each job before moving on to step 2, weighing your options. When you have a few jobs to decide on, do this process and look at the scores. Out of the current options, choose the job with the highest score because for now, it's what comes closest to your ideal. If this leads you to your ideal job that you didn't know was out there before—fantastic. If you still remain unsatisfied, you may have to go one step deeper and create something that doesn't yet exist.

Exercise: Find or create the dream job

My dad used to say, "Figure out how many hours a week you are willing to work. If you don't have a job, then spend that amount of time looking for work." I'm not certain we always have the luxury to do this (certainly if you are unemployed you can), but if you are looking for work on top of your other job or jobs, it may be confusing to decide how much time to spend on this.

Start by spending 10% of your weekly work hours toward looking for a new job. If you're not in a job at all, the gathering of information is your full time job. Do whatever it takes. Look online for 90 minutes every night. Interview on a weekend. If you are referred to a job fair, go! Ask questions of your employed friends. Ask questions of your satisfied friends. You might find the ideal match but not be chosen to do the job. Maybe this is opening the door for something else.

If you're unable to find your dream job, spend this time creating a list of the qualities of your dream job and research what it would take to bring your vision into existence. If it doesn't light up your heart, it isn't your dream job. Keep looking.

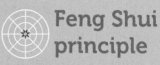

Health and Balance

"Health is a state of complete harmony of the body, mind and spirit. When one is free from physical disabilities and mental distractions, the gates of the soul open." — K.S. Iyengar

HOW WE DEFINE HEALTH

In the West, we tend to view health as an absence of symptoms or disease. In the East, health is viewed as the strength of our overall system, an integration and harmony of the whole body, the mind and our levels of energy (or chi.) In one case, the focus is on the *lack* of negativity; in the other, the focus is on the *presence* of vitality.

So what does it mean to be healthy? To some people, it means a variation on "not being sick." To other people, it means being a quick healer. Others still think it means having a glow about you, or bright, clean eyes and a strong

Feng Shui principle

The fourth ancient Hawaiian Huna secret is 'Manawa,' which means "Now is the moment of power." There is nothing that exists outside of this moment. Anything else is a memory or a future projection. There is only now.

Color your world

Colors that correspond with vibrant health are grand golds, bright oranges and vivid reds. Good support colors are deep pinks, shades of brown and any other earth tones that make you feel grounded.

spirit. But where does health begin?

In 1948, the World Health Assembly defined health as "a state of complete physical, mental and social well-being and not merely the absence of disease or infirmity."

What are the characteristics that create the state of well-being? It isn't dissimilar to the qualities we look to create within a home. If you ask people the characteristics they notice after they feng shui their space, the response is often balance, harmony and flow. Would it surprise you to learn that these principles work within the body as well?

BALANCE

The symbol for balance in feng shui is the yin yang. It represents the harmonious co-existence of opposites. In fact, one definition for balance reads: "A harmonious or satisfying arrangement or proportion of parts or elements, as in a design." These principles can also contribute to a sense of health and well-being.

HARMONY

The concept of harmony speaks to all of the elements or items working together in a way that provides positive results. One definition for harmony is a pleasing combination of elements in a whole. When things work in harmony with one another, the individual elements rise above and become a sum greater than their parts.

FLOW

When things are blocked, cluttered or jammed, there is no room for movement. When things stagnate inside the body or mind, they begin to rot, creating a breeding ground for disease. One definition for flow is "to circulate, as the blood in the body." You can imagine how beneficial this can be in so many aspects of our health: proper digestion, breathing deeply and sweating out toxins.

To sum it up, health is having a body that contains the states of balance, harmony and flow. Disease occurs when things are out of balance, where there is a breakdown of communication within the body, and when things such as blood or even negative emotions stagnate. It seems that there are three main systems where these qualities come into play with regard to health: the physical body, the mind and the energetic system, or "spirit."

OUR PHYSICAL BODY

Within the body, there are many delicate and intricate systems at play. It's a very western approach to try and break these systems down into separate categories; however, they are all interconnected. There are different ways to look at the body as a complete health system.

HANGING IN THE BALANCE

When there are imbalances inside the body, they can lead to disease. Here are a few different ways of assessing the balance of health:

The ph (acid/alkali) balance The human body maintains a normal overall pH range of 7.35-7.45. Although both acidity and alkalinity exist within the body, when imbalanced, trouble emerges. A relatively recent concept in the field of natural healthcare, the pH or acid-alkali balance of the body has an impact on almost every aspect of well-being and health. Too much acidity is a major factor in congestion and inflammation, it weakens the immune system and aggravates most chronic conditions. Body pH is affected by what we eat and is key in preventative medicine.

Ayurveda-The Science of Life In India, there is a system of medicine called Ayurveda, whose founding principles are balance and moderation. According to this system, there are certain mind and body types called Doshas. The three types are Vata, Pitta and Kapha. If one is more dominant in your system, this imbalance can cause discord (lack of harmony) in the system, leading to disease.

Chinese Medicine In Traditional Chinese Medicine (TCM), there are four groups of opposites used to diagnose disease. Yin and yang, cold and heat, internal and external, deficiency and excess. When these systems remain in balance and harmony, the body is considered to be in a state of health. When they fall out of balance, discord follows just as the moon follows the sun.

Life in the west In western living, we get into trouble when we live lives of excess or malnourishment. When we eat too much sugar or don't get enough healthy fats, we create disease. When we overeat or starve ourselves, we cause bodily harm. We hear about people whose blood pressure is too low and others whose blood pressure is too high. When pathogens (bacteria and viruses) run amok in the body, it creates an increase of white blood cells to help get them under control.

All of these systems reflect the fact that nature correlates balance with health. By looking at the body as a whole, we can create a healthy balance and work to avoid things that throw it off balance.

The six essentials for life

Our pH balance can be affected by everything from what we eat and drink and breathe as well as the exercise we do, the thoughts we think and how we sleep. Dr. M.T. Morter, Jr. created the Morter Health System, a complete system of healthcare based on Bio Energetic Synchronization Technique, a nutrition program based on acid/alkaline balance and guidelines for making correct choices in the Six Essentials of Life. The six essentials are what you eat, what you drink, how you exercise, how you rest, what you breathe and what you think. For more information, go to morter.com/six.php.

GET THINGS FLOWING

Exercise gets the blood flowing in the body. Blood flow helps deliver oxygen and nutrients to parts of the body that need it. Blood also carts away toxins to our inner recycling and waste removal systems. When the body sits for extended periods of time, we become sluggish, which can affect our mood, brain function and immune systems.

Exercise is obviously an essential part of staying healthy. Getting your sweat on can help keep the skin healthy and flush toxins out of the body so they don't need to come out of the lungs or waste system. It isn't always clear what the best exercises are for us, so listen to your own body.

One thing to consider is contra-lateral exercise. This is where you work out opposite sides of the body simultaneously. Take walking for example: as your right leg swings forward, so does your left arm; then the left leg swings forward at the same time as the right arm. If your focus is on the communication within the body, walk empty handed so that there is a balance in the signals being sent back and forth. Swimming is another excellent contra-lateral exercise, as is yoga. These forms of exercise can increase the flow of communication between both sides of the brain, communication up and down the spinal column and communication between both sides of the body, helping your coordination and reflexes.

Another thing that relates to flow is the amount of water we have in our bodies. You need to make sure that you are getting enough water, otherwise you could get dehydrated. The human body is made up of anywhere from 55% -78% water, and if it's in the right balance, it can help cellular function and communication. In this case, balance leads to flow and flow leads to harmony.

My personal story: I used to avoid getting up in the middle of the night to go to the bathroom, mostly because I hate, more than almost anything, the feeling of having to pee. But I also hated the feeling of getting up, walking to the bathroom and coming back to bed, because I felt like I never got a deep night's sleep after I did. When choosing between the two, I created a win-lose. I'd either have to pee, and that would affect my dreams, or I'd go to the bathroom and then not sleep as deeply as I wished. Over time, I just avoided liquid for hours before bed. As a result, I think

I walked around for years being dehydrated. In fact, my doctor tested me and told me I was dehydrated and explained the importance of water in creating something called intra-cellular communication, the energy that gets passed between cells.

I had to find a solution that was no longer win-lose. The solution came from a naturopath named Sharyn Wynters. She suggested adding a supplement of electrolytes to my daily dose of water. I could drink much less liquid and wouldn't have to constantly get up to pee. That was my win-win.

YOUR INNER ECOLOGY

My friend Randy created and ran a tonic bar at a natural food market (Erewhon) near my house in Los Angeles. He was the one who first introduced me to the concept of inner ecology. The more he talked about it, the more it sounded like feng shui for your body. This idea was reiterated by Sharyn Wynters when she said food has several purposes. Some foods cleanse, some foods balance and some foods nourish. Sounds a lot like feng shui to me.

A few inner ecology principles are:

> 1. Our body is an ecosystem. Everything you bring into your space (including what was there before you started being responsible for the space) has an impact on you. This is true in feng shui as well. In many ways, our body is like a home. And in many ways, people's homes become "sick."

2. Health is related to having a balance inside as well as out. Doing a cleanse can help reduce the "stuff" (toxicity) that's inside our body, which can help bring our acid/alkaline back into balance. It is essential to maintain balance in feng shui, because when things are in balance, the environment is more likely to promote and sustain life.

3. We want to add more things into our space that help to promote life. This can range from live foods to probiotics. In feng shui there are things we can bring into the environment that help to promote life as well. To have more life in our lives sets the stage for us to be more alive, to have more health and to have a better experience each and every day we live in that space.

CREATE PHYSICAL HARMONY

One of the ways to create harmony in the body is to become aware of what we eat. Further, we may want to become familiar with a process called "food combining." This refers to specific combinations of foods that are compatible with each other in terms of digestive chemistry. Food combining is an essential component of optimal nutrition because it allows our bodies to digest and use the nutrients in our food to the greatest possible extent. Inner body chemistry can relate to inner harmony and well-being.

Another way to create harmony in the body is to allow the body to rest deeply and fully. As Emerson said, "Health is the first muse and

Food combining

Food combining (also known as trophology) describes how certain combinations of food result in improper digestion, and the food decays in the gut. When this happens, toxins are released instead of allowing nutrients to be absorbed.

The ancient Chinese were well aware of the importance of the science of food combining. The following advice was given to the founding emperor of the Ming Dynasty on his 100th birthday: "Food and drink are relied upon to nurture life. But if one does not know that the nature of substances may be opposed to each other, and one consumes them altogether indiscriminately, the vital organs will be thrown out of harmony and disastrous consequences will soon arise. Therefore, those who wish to nurture their lives must carefully avoid doing such damage to themselves."

—Chia Ming, Essential Knowledge for Eating and Drinking, 1368 A.D.

sleep is the condition to produce it." During sleep, there are many things happening simultaneously. Our organs are on their own schedules, and nighttime is when they take out the trash. Our minds get quiet and all the information from our day is processed while we dream. Our batteries are being recharged as we reconnect with our source. When our sleep cycle gets interrupted, it can impede the body's natural ability to regulate and rejuvenate.

Ultimately, our ability to heal and stay strong will depend greatly on the cultivation of these three qualities of balance, flow and harmony within our bodies. But as we will soon find out, they extend beyond the physical body as well.

OUR MENTAL BODY

The mind is powerful in its ability to help us boost our immune systems, keep us healthy and help us recuperate from disease. Choose your thoughts wisely. As Alison Rose Levy said in *An Ancient Cure for Modern Life*: "In minds crammed with thoughts, organs clogged with toxins and bodies stiffened with neglect, there is just no space for anything else."

Imbalance in the brain is the equivalent of a car that overheats. Perhaps we are thinking too much. We spend so much time thinking and utilizing our bodies from the neck up that sometimes we need to just "get out of our heads" for a while. This doesn't simply mean stopping thinking, but includes the rest of the body, too. Exercise can be very good for the physical body, but it can also affect our mental body as well.

The way we exercise can be as important as what we do. What do you think about while you exercise? Do you read trashy magazines? Are you looking at pictures of other people's bodies? Whether you are looking at bodies that you would like, or bodies that are not as good as yours, you are likely doing a lot of comparing.

People often watch TV, listen to music or daydream during their workout. While this can provide you with a necessary break from your nagging thoughts, focusing on these external things might make our workout less efficient, and might distract you enough that you get hurt. Plus, if you are watching someone else in yoga, you're probably not remembering to breathe.

Studies have shown that the more focused you are, the less exercise you need to do. Being mindful helps strengthen the mind-body connection. Ultimately, being present in your workout should help with balance, coordination and regeneration.

The state of being that is most similar to the deepest stages of rest is meditation. This doesn't just mean sitting cross-legged and staring at a candle. I generally break meditations down into two types: passive meditations and active meditations.

Passive meditations are where we simply observe what is. We may observe the river of our thoughts. We may focus on one thing, such as our breath, a candle or a repetitive sound. Sometimes the goal is to trying to empty out our thoughts until there is nothing left.

Examples of more active meditation are when we chant, do yoga, run, dance, clean the house, drive a car for long distances or make love. These actions can actually quiet the mind. After these activities, you may notice a deeper, more profound silence than you have ever experienced.

Sometimes it's nice to use a guided meditation. There are CD's available that are just a few minutes or longer. Your only job is to close your eyes, follow along and visualize. It's a different experience than listening to your inner guidance. It depends on what type of meditation you are craving. Regardless of the type of meditation, see if you can create a few seconds of focused attention before you lose your focus. Start small and build up: 30 seconds; 2 minutes; 5 minutes; one hour. Play around and see what works for you.

As you meditate, some things may come up. You may notice that your mind is going a mile a minute. This is generally when many people judge what they're doing and decide that they aren't having a successful meditation. One suggestion in these moments is to try to be like an observer of what is happening, rather than feeling as though it is happening to you. There is no requirement for you to do anything about it. Just to be present. Really listen to each question that's coming up. Don't try to answer them, just listen as if your mind is that of a six-year old child who needs to be heard for a little while. Eventually you may just pass out from exhaustion and need a nap.

If you notice your mind is in a circular line of questioning or obsessed with a nagging negative thought, then change the channel. (This is like the orange water that comes out of the tap when you first turn it on; see "Your Inner Radio," pg. 63, in chapter 3 for a reminder). As we learned in

The Dalai Lama was asked what surprised him the most; he said:

"Man, because he sacrifices his health in order to make money. Then he sacrifices money to recuperate his health. And then he is so anxious about the future that he does not enjoy the present; the result being that he does not live in the present or the future; he lives as if he is never going to die, and then he dies having never really lived."

previous chapters: *nature abhors a vacuum,* so you may need to choose something to focus on. Try alternating between a passive meditation where you are just receiving whatever happens and a more active meditation where you choose something to occupy your mind.

A benefit of meditation is that it balances both sides if the brain. Studies have been done where they noticed that the part of the brain that connects both hemispheres is much stronger and more developed in monks who meditate every day for hours.

Earlier in life, I had a different concept of meditation than the concept I have of it today. It seemed harder, more foreign and I couldn't get my brain to shut up. It took meeting a Feng Shui master to get me interested in understanding how meditation affects my energy, not to mention my mind and my body.

I've now had an ongoing meditation practice since 2003. It's not daily, but it's consistent. Some of my best ideas come after or during my meditation and when I've done chanting meditation, I feel something happening. Later, when good things happen (more opportunities, increased energy, clearer mental focus), it confirms that my actions had a tangible effect on my life. An unforeseen byproduct of doing this meditation is that I've developed a tremendous amount of confidence in my ability to do something consistently for 40 days. That confidence has opened up what I'm able to commit to in my life, including marriage and being responsible for another person. Originally I was just doing it to quiet my mind, but I realized this great benefit from it.

Another benefit of meditation is that it can put us in harmony with the world around us. By meditating, we tap into our inner wisdom and the collective unconscious. Some people feel they are drawn closer to God. Insights that come out of the silence and hints of intuition you follow up on will most likely result in serendipity, happy accidents, etc. You are now in the flow of life. Enjoy!

Being negative One of the obstacles to flow is negativity. Computer programmers use the term GIGO, or Garbage in, garbage out. Whatever you put in will be processed and come back to you. Thoughts of worry, fear and doubt slow down our flow and bring it to a screeching halt. As much as possible, see if you can stay focused on positive thoughts. They will attract more of the same and end up being more helpful than being negative ever will.

I read an article recently that said that luck was an easy skill to learn by choosing to be positive. People who focused on negative things didn't even notice the opportunities that came their way; they were too busy focusing on what they were worried about. I've had several teachers throughout my life that have demonstrated for me how to look for the good in a situation and how important it is to work that skill as if it were a muscle, almost right away after an experience.

One of these teachers was Dr. Renata Mihalic, the chiropractor I started going to about a year after my mom passed away. She helped me start to work that muscle—seeing the positive in my life after a trauma left me feeling like I might never find the good again. Practice makes us stronger. Using that mental muscle is now a regular part of my daily practice.

There is nothing outside of now Other obstacles to flow are future thinking and holding on to the past. Another reason to meditate is that it can help bring us back into the moment. Mentioned at the beginning of this chapter was the idea that you can change your entire life in *this moment*. Try changing the past, or going into the future and doing something to guarantee an outcome. Nothing can change your relationship to your own past or influence the future like what you are capable of in this very moment. As Jonathan Larson wrote in the musical *Rent*, "There's only us. There's only this. Forget regret. Or life is yours to miss. No other road. No other way. No day but today."

MENTAL STRESS

Thinking about the past and the future can create a feeling of overwhelm in the present. Being overwhelmed creates a considerable amount of internal stress. Stress and harmony are antithetical to one another. When we are stressed, we lose the feeling of connectedness to the rest of the world.

In this moment, we just have to take one step. It gives us clarity to be able to put everything into perspective and not get overwhelmed by the whole process. Another benefit of being in the moment is that you get to know yourself better, and it's likely that if you listen to your inner self, over time you're going to have more authentic experiences. The decisions you make from a place of authenticity will be more harmonious than the ones that come from fear. When we feel connected to the magic of the world, we feel healthier and more alive.

OUR SPIRIT BODY

In Chinese medicine, there is an energy called chi (also spelled Qi; both are pronounced chee), which flows in nature, in our homes and in our bodies. There are two kinds of chi: Sha Chi and Sheng Chi. Sha chi can be stagnant or destructive. The simplest definition of Sheng Chi is positive energy. For a more harmonious life, I recommend that you cultivate Sheng Chi both outside in your space and within yourself.

ENERGETIC BALANCE

You may not be able to see chi, but an acupuncturist can tell you what's going on by listening to your pulse. The point of acupuncture is that we can access meridians of energy that run throughout our system. When they are balanced and energy is flowing, then harmony follows, helping ensure health and longevity. When imbalanced, we experience negative symptoms such as pain, discomfort or disease.

Invisible bandits There are other invisible imbalanced elements that can influence us, such as free radicals. Just because you don't see them doesn't mean they aren't affecting you. This is the cumulative effect of having computers, WiFi, satellites, cell phones, microwaves and other electronics placed throughout our homes and offices. They can create free radicals, which are unstable molecules known to cause tissue damage and enhance the effects of aging.

The antidote is to surround yourself with negative ions. Thought by some to be the vitamins of the air, negative ions (in this case, negative is a good thing!) are found in nature, where wind blows through the trees, where ocean meets rock and after a rainstorm. If you can't get to nature, your shower at home contains a natural supply of negative ions. You can also create them by placing Himalayan rock salt lamps or burning beeswax candles within your space. The key is to get out into nature as much as possible or work to bring nature home with you.

ENERGETIC FLOW

The energy of emotions Some people refer to emotions as energy in motion. If we repress our emotions, we may get depressed. Over time, stuck emotions might even contribute to the suppression of our immune system, which can lead to disease. We know that food affects our mind and our mind creates emotions, but our emotions can also affect our thoughts and the ability of the body to do its job. When we allow emotions to flow, energy can move again. Stuck energy can get placed into parts of the body where it doesn't belong. Emotions can be stored and even digested in certain organs in the body. This can cause our system to give certain signals at the wrong time and throw off the energy grid in our bodies, much like creating a traffic jam inside a major city. Confronting your feelings and letting them out actually frees up energy within the body. This energy can be used for other essential body functions.

Martial Arts, Chi Gong and Reiki There are ways to cultivate your own good energy. You can study a martial art form that puts an emphasis on breathing and chi-building techniques. You can study Chi Gong or Tai Chi Ch'uan, which help to energize the body, flooding it with chi (also known as ki in Japan, prana in India and mana in Hawaii.) You can also study Reiki (Rei'ki), which helps to balance the electromagnetic field of the body and is being used in hospitals on patients to help them relax.

ENERGETIC HARMONY

The word yoga means union. It means union with the divine and union with everyone and everything around you. When we do yoga, we are working out our physical body, but we are also balancing our chakras, which represent our energy system. Yoga is not just about physical postures, but also about breathing techniques, chanting and singing and certain ways of being in the world that can help us transform our energy and feel harmony with the rest of the world.

You don't even have to practice yoga to "do yoga." I've heard yoga teachers describe yoga as a metaphor, saying that true yoga is living our lives out in the world. If you do wish to explore energy systems, the yoga room is an excellent place to start thinking about your world. Pretty soon everything will have an underpinning of energy and your perspective will never be the same.

Misery loves company The old adage goes: "Show me your friends and I'll show you who you are." This is true, because we end up absorbing the energy of those who we spend time with. This is why is feels so good to be around positive, uplifting folks, or the "Tiggers" of the world. It is also why it can be a real bummer to be around realists and pessimists, or the "Eeyores" of the world. Be careful who you spend your time with and who you are committed to being.

Harmony with the world around you I think everyone knows what it feels like to be in harmony with the world, like when you're playing with an animal or a child and you get lost and time flies. Or when

EXERCISE: Address all three bodies (physical/mental/spiritual)
Draw a bath and put in some sea salts. (Sea salts are excellent for leaching out toxins, replacing essential minerals, relaxing the mind and cleansing our energy.) Before you get in the bath, spend 30 seconds focusing on your intention. Then allow yourself to take a deep breath and hold it as long as you can. As you exhale, let go of everything that is currently a stress to you—situations, people, recurring thoughts or worries. Let them all go. Spend nine breaths doing this. You are making space. If you're really worked up about something, you can write in a journal or talk to God. Just get out whatever is inside, whatever you are holding on to. Let it go.

The second half is about receiving. Start by listening. Listen to all of the sounds—constant sounds, your heartbeat, anything you notice—and just see what comes. A vision. A feeling. A sound or phrase or song. You've made space; now just receive. Be open to being surprised. And when you are done, give a little thanks. It will set your body to a high frequency for whatever is next, even if you just go to bed.

you're on a date and it's so great that you just enjoy being in that person's presence. Or when you get a runner's high. We all know that feeling, but as adults we tend to forget (mostly because we're living from our neck up too much of the time.) Living in the moment is synonymous with being a whole person in a whole body and being connected to all of its parts. Dance. Savor each bite of a meal. Play! Before you know it, you'll feel back in harmony with the world around you.

FULL CIRCLE

Our mental body and our energy body can in turn affect our physical body. I know that I started talking about the physical body first, then the thought body and finally the energy body, but it can work the other way too. Sometimes the mental clutter and the emotional blockages can manifest physically. Not only with regard to disease, but also putting and keeping weight on. It's usually not recommended by people who practice mindfulness to focus on losing weight. The idea is that focusing on what you don't want (in this case, what you want to lose) keeps affirming the weight you want to get rid of. Instead, make your physical home replicate what you see in your mind and add power to it with your emotions. Picture a lighter body, connected to the world and energized by it. Feel peace and joy course through your veins. All of these things can happen in an instant. If you walk around feeling peaceful and joyful most of the time, that weight will find its way off. You'll have less cravings, your immune system will respond to those higher-vibrational thoughts and you'll feel motivated to do physical activity. Overall, it's a win-win.

Family and Past

"He that is discontented in one place will seldom be happy in another."

— Aesop

Feng Shui principle

Ideally, we seek to set our physical spaces up so that we are in a position of power. We want something strong supporting us, like a mountain at our back. Whether it is literal or metaphoric, we always want to ask, "Who has my back?"

WHERE WE COME FROM AFFECTS WHERE WE ARE GOING

In feng shui, the family area represents our past, our foundation and the area that "has our back." When we feel that something has our back, we feel supported and the world is safer. Think about how you view the world. Is it inherently friendly? Or is everyone out to get you? How you answer this question has to do with the filter through which you look at the world. What creates this filter? The past. Our experience of the past colors the way we view things that come into our life. The unknown either represents

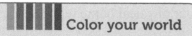

Color your world

The best colors for honoring our past and our family are those that represent the element wood. In feng shui, forest green, rich jade and healing sage are all good support colors. You can also bring in blacks, deep blues and combinations of blue and green together, such as teal. Since green is the color that relates to the heart chakra, it can help support healing on the deepest level.

new opportunities, or untold dangers that put us on high alert.

When your back faces a room, you may find yourself looking over your shoulder a lot, especially every time you feel something or hear a noise. This is a good thing, because it's in our DNA to make sure we are safe. However, the feeling that something is wrong activates a fight-or-flight reflex in our bodies, which can drain us over the long haul. Feeling anxious all the time makes the body produce hormones that are good if you need to lift a car off of your child, but over the long run, they can wear out your adrenal glands and suppress your immune system, leaving you susceptible to illness.

Whether we are talking about someone literally having your back (like a bodyguard) or metaphorically having your back, we need to feel safe in the world if we are going to thrive. Sometimes these influences are happening outside the realm of our conscious mind.

CORE BELIEFS

Our family or primary caregivers help to create our core beliefs, most of which were created by our perception of life growing up. These core beliefs tell a story which colors the way we look at the world. No matter how much we avoid looking at these beliefs, they eventually resurface. As the old maxim says: "Wherever you go, there you are."

Why are some of us afraid of the dark? Because in the dark, you can't see, so you are forced to imagine what is out there. Our imagination is projected onto the unknown, which becomes something exciting or something scary. The unknown can be friend or it can be foe, but our response to it reflects our deepest thoughts about ourselves and our place in the world. As Nietzsche said, "If you stare into the abyss long enough, the abyss stares back at you." The universe can be a scary place if our relationship to our past is unresolved. There may be things we do within our control that perpetuate a sense of things from our past still being unresolved. One example might be avoiding uncomfortable conversations because you don't know how they will turn out.

For the longest time, I've had a lot of "charge" about my name. Back story: My birth name was Ariel, with a different middle name (Jonas) and last name (Fagin) than I currently have. My mother was married to my biological father, Sanford Fagin, for only the first nine months of my life. In the hospital, my mother was pressured to give me a name right away, even though you technically have 30 days to name your baby. She always placed a high significance on what goes into a name. She herself felt compelled to change her birth name to a chosen artist name, which she went by for the rest of her life. She told an interesting story about the day it happened. She heard a deep inner voice that urged her to consider this new name; she liked the name, and from that point on, she went by Crystal Star.

I had a similar experience when I was 5 years old and I was playing at school. By this time, my mom had remarried and was now with my stepdad, Joe Towne. When I came home from school that day, I jumped into the car and announced to them that I wanted to change my name to little Joe. My stepdad was big Joe, he had been in my life since I was 1 ½ years old, and

"So I've started being vigilant about watching my thoughts all day, monitoring them. I repeat this vow about 700 times a day: 'I will not harbor unhealthy thoughts anymore.' Every time a diminishing thought arises, I repeat the vow.

I will not harbor unhealthy thoughts anymore. The first time I heard myself say this, my inner ear perked up at the word 'harbor', which is a noun as well as a verb. A harbor, of course, is a place of refuge, a port of entry...

You may not come here anymore with your hard and abusive thoughts, with your plague ships of thoughts, with your slave ships of thoughts, with your warships of thoughts – all these will be turned away...Cannibalistic thoughts, for obvious reasons, will no longer be received. Even missionaries will be carefully screened, for sincerity. This is a peaceful harbor, the entryway to a fine and proud island that is only now beginning to cultivate tranquility. If you can abide by these new laws, my dear thoughts, then you are welcome in my mind – otherwise I shall turn you back toward the sea from whence you came. That is my mission, and it will never end."

—Elizabeth Gilbert, Eat Pray Love

he felt the most like a dad. Needless to say, they both said yes.

This decision really hurt my biological father, who I visited every other weekend. For many years, he believed it wasn't my decision, but that it was the influence of my mom and stepdad trying to put a divide between us. I carried a lot of guilt and worry about my name. On one hand, I was a hippie kid from Long Island who was trying to grow up in the 80's with the name of a Shakespearean sprite, and on the other hand, I just wanted to fit in and the name Joe allowed me to do that very easily. It wasn't until right after I graduated college that I finally started to make peace with my birth name, after going by my stepdad's name for 15 years, all through school and college. When I finally merged them both together into a name of my choosing, Ariel Joseph Towne, I immediately felt like things started to move forward for me in a different way than I had experienced before. I no longer felt an inner split, and I legally changed my name a few years later, following in the footsteps of my mom. Balance achieved.

The universe can be a scary place if our relationships to the past are unresolved. For such a long time, I had unresolved feelings around my name, and as a result, I kind of felt like two people. One person when I visited one side of my family, and another when I visited the other side of my family. It was almost like one version of me was cheating on the other, and if I enjoyed one too much, I felt guilty. But mostly it was the name that I had chosen that I felt guilty about. That's when I decided I had to tell my biological father that I had legally changed my name. Once I did and stated my choice, it helped free me from all that guilt and core belief that I'd been carrying around for such a long time. My old core belief was that I could never be seen for who I truly was; I felt like there was always something I would have to hide behind. But I didn't create those circumstances by myself; everyone played their role in their opinions about my name, but I did try and change those circumstances by claiming my own name for myself, which is something most children don't do. Since then, I've formed a different belief, which is that I can be seen for who I truly am.

GOSSIP AND THE PERPETUATION OF SUFFERING

Let's say you scrape your knee. It hurts, and in the moment, you are uncomfortable, but know it will heal over time. To your body, it may eventually be like the knee scrape never happened. What if you tell the story of your injury to everyone you know in order to elicit sympathy?

On one level, you may hear comforting words, which temporarily make you feel better, but that's not going to make you heal any faster, and studies have shown that your body can't tell the difference between the event happening and your brain imagining it. If you re-tell a sob story ten times, it's like you've just relived it ten times, so consider what that is doing to your body each time you say it. First, you are releasing hormones into your system that affect your body chemistry and need to be processed. Second, the more connections your memories have, the better chance that a neural pathway will lead to that memory. Repeated reliving of a memory enhances its permanence. And third, the emotional trauma that the memory brings up has to be processed and released as well.

We don't have to be stoic and repress everything that happens to us, but we can be selective about what we share and how often. I'm sure we've all known someone who seems to play the victim. It's almost as if part of them cannot let it go. Most of their stories circle back to some aspect of their past that they are having trouble letting go of. These people are being defined by their past in a way that makes it difficult for them to move forward. As my teacher Yasuhiko would say, "It is not the pain, but the story we tell about our pain that perpetuates our suffering." Each story we share can be a weight off our shoulders, or one more that we pile on to be dealt with at a later time.

I have several clients, who, after a breakup, tend to tell the story over and over again to anyone who will listen. I know they're doing this because they want sympathy and that sympathy is designed to put out the fire of their pain, but there is another way. There's a way to process the pain and not perpetuate our suffering. What we're focusing on grows in our experiences. Recreating the circumstances in our mind forces some part of us to repeat it, which might in turn create more opportunities to attract that experience. It's like the saying "What you think about, you bring about."

How we treat our pain might vary from person to person. It might require some TLC, some distractions and, most of all, time. Recreating the past doesn't seem to do anything other than make us relive it. Instead, (and this is one of the hardest things in the world to do) if possible, focus on something that was great about the relationship and choose that to take forward. Regardless of the circumstances of the breakup, ultimately, it's important to accept the breakup and eventually take something good from it. Do you want to take a story of how you were victimized or a story of how you were loved? Which feels like a more empowering story moving into the future: One in which things don't work out, or one in which they did, if only for a time?

HOW YOUR PAST AFFECTS YOUR PRESENT

Let's imagine that every experience we have is recorded on a little CD in our brain that influences our muscle memory and our energy field. These memories can be replayed if something triggers them. While we dream, the grandmaster DJ of our minds chooses which discs it wants to play. If a memory plays on repeat over and over again, it can cause certain physical reactions: reinforcing the way our body holds onto it, increasing the amount of times we think of it, and dredging up negative associations that we have with it. The result: more resentment, more sadness, and more victimization in our waking life. If we recognize that something from our past is clouding our present-day experiences, we may need to work to identify what that is. Only once we *realize* our pattern can we *choose* something different.

One of my stories from the past that kept interrupting my present was about how my family never made money doing what they loved, and eventually, I watched them all stop pursuing those careers. As you can imagine, it can be really difficult if you don't have any examples to follow of how things can work out. You probably default to how they won't.

My example was that you can't make money doing what you love to do, which was demonstrated by both my mom and my dad. My mom was an artist and my dad was a radio DJ. Whenever I would struggle financially, my father's advice always seemed to be rooted in the core belief you can't make money doing what you love to do. My mom, on the other hand, would encourage me in my artistic endeavors, but she was no longer pursuing her own artistic dream. She put it aside in order to put food on the table. These examples so permeated my childhood, it was really challenging for me to break through and accept the possibility of what I'd never seen intellectually, felt emotionally or been gifted energetically.

It was up to me to transform this pattern. It really can be challenging to overcome what feels like a spiritual legacy, but if you work at it, stay focused and give yourself a good role model of what is possible, thoughts can start to circulate around that instead of the old story. It's about healing the underlying past core belief and old story to make room for something new.

I don't blame my dad; he was taught those beliefs by his dad, who was probably taught them by his father. It was a different era; they were worried about war and depression, and they didn't have the hope that came with the 70's. I don't blame my mother either. I'm so thankful that she at least gave me the emotional support possible to take a leap into the unknown and change my pattern.

I love the quote that says, "If I'm anything, it's because I've stood on the shoulders of giants." My mother taught me that anything was possible, and my dad shared his worry about what might not happen. Sometimes we are encouraged to reach for what is possible, and sometimes we learn by railing against the impossible. My parents were both inspirations to me in their own way.

ROCKS IN YOUR BACKPACK

In feng shui, we say, "you can't pick up something new in your life unless you put down what you are holding on to." In this case, what we are holding onto can take different shapes and appear in different ways, but they each weigh us down as if we were wearing backpacks filled with stones from our past. These rocks include, but are not limited to, fears, guilt, debts, resentments or injustices.

Fear The things we are afraid of weigh us down. They keep us chasing shadows and endlessly preparing for what may lay ahead. Most of the things we worry about don't come to fruition. The things that do, we get to say "I told you so." But on some level, we may worry that we helped bring it into being with our negative thinking.

Guilt The things we cannot forgive ourselves for cause guilt to weigh heavily on our hearts. Some health experts say that guilt can bring about

Healing Back Pain: The Mind-Body Connection
by John E. Sarno, M.D.

According to Dr. Sarno, there is a clear mind-body connection when it comes to back pain. Recurring ailments in the body sometimes start as something psychological that may have happened a long time ago. It may be difficult to see the direct correlation, but it's possible that there is a connection between the pain and something unresolved in our lives. Unfortunately, we tend to get used to the pain signals over time, which makes it harder to identify with feelings of peace and ease. Sometimes we have to do a little digging and notice what is causing the stress on the body. By releasing what we are holding onto, we can clear the way for a strong, healthy back.

disease, make us feel profound embarrassment or make us want to be invisible. We may not feel worthy of much of anything if we believe in our own guilt over a situation.

Debts When we owe someone something, it can create an awful feeling. We may feel shame if we have trouble repaying our debts in a timely fashion. We may feel hopeless, as if we will never be free from our obligations. People who have debts tend to have core beliefs of unworthiness or a profound sense of not being "enough."

Resentments/Injustices Resentments can fester over time. Unless we learn to speak up, we may carry this burden as it slowly burns a hole in our hearts. The damage created from resentments can end relationships and indicate a lack of ability to share and hold the truth with one another. There are very few ways that resentment can be healed completely. No amount of time seems to transform it on its own, but there are things you can do to encourage the healing process.

If you recognize things in your past that you're clinging to, you can lighten the load by finding ways to release unwanted stuff (such as the sacred fire exercise at the end of Chapter 3 and the forgiveness ritual at the end of this chapter.) Once you release these things, you will have more energy to move forward. If you don't release them, they can have emotional, mental and physical repercussions.

YOUR COMMUNITY OF SUPPORT

A spiritual principle is: wherever two or more are gathered in the name of something, the more powerful it is, so consider gathering support from others when working to manifest something close to your heart. Maybe it's the creation of a Mastermind group, or sharing your vision with a couple of close friends or family members. Having this safety net is an important thing; if your foundation is shaky, it's hard to rely on it, but if your foundation is solid, it's a great place to build upon.

Be very careful whom you invite into this innermost circle. If you talk to a positive person who has no attachment to your dreams, you'll probably get a different response than if you share with a really negative person who may unconsciously sabotage your efforts. The negative person may not be malicious in their intent; they could just be afraid of being left alone if you accomplish your dreams. Discretion is the name of the game.

There are two main categories of people that make up our "family." First there are people you are energetically connected to, people who share your physical DNA. This includes all of your ancestors and blood relatives. The second group includes the people who may not share blood but who have been instrumental in your development: family through marriage, teachers, caretakers and employees, friends' parents, mentors and whoever you spend time with that had an important part in developing your core beliefs about yourself.

Another realm of support are those whom we consider to be our chosen families. These are the people who come into our lives and who we carry with us in our hearts; our closest friends and deepest confidantes. We might even refer to these people as our "soul family" because it can feel as though they have come into our lives for a deeper purpose.

In 2006, my dad was hospitalized very suddenly. Without warning, it seemed that his life was on the line and he didn't have a way out. He had an aortic dissection. He experienced a major shredding of his aortic valve and was on life support. Miracle workers at NYU medical center kept him alive, albeit on life support.

The first thing that I thought to do was to form a prayer group with anyone I knew who believed in something. It didn't matter to me what who they were or what they believed in; what mattered to me was that they believed. I wrote to them about the situation and simply asked them to send their energy toward whatever my dad wanted and whatever his spirit wanted. Since he was on a breathing tube and unconscious, I couldn't communicate with him. I asked the group to send their thoughts supporting my dad if he wanted to stay, and supporting a peaceful and painless transition if he wanted to go. I wrote to them every day about his updates and progress. Two months later, my dad walked out of the hospital to the surprise of everyone, including his doctors and nurses. I'm convinced that this prayer group combined with his desire to live (and the team of nurses and doctors who, despite their reservations, worked tirelessly to save his life) helped create what doctors call the miraculous recovery.

THINK LIKE A TREE

The family area is represented by the element wood and its symbol is the tree. A tree can only grow as high as its roots are deep. If your relationship to your past is limiting your ability to move forward, you may want to address some aspect of your past that is still bothering you.

Ensure that your soil is free from weeds (or unhealthy thoughts which crop up from time to time). Infuse your tree with elements that can help it thrive, such as sunlight (the light of your consciousness), water (the

Body Talk

Several clients/colleagues of mine are BodyTalk practitioners. I have experienced sessions many times and have had some interesting results from the work. The premise is that we can self-heal if we can get out of our own way and release the blocks that prevent healing. These practitioners have shared with me several examples of imbalance: emotions being stored in our liver and kidneys, being digested in our stomach (places where emotions shouldn't be), or our body may be sending the right signal at the wrong time. When things are imbalanced, it's as if our internal wires are crossed. BodyTalk allows a practitioner to "speak" to our bodies and ask what needs to be released to allow for optimal self-care and maintenance.

Whether it is this or another method of healing, check in and see what feels right to you. Talk to people about what you're passionate about and that will probably lead you to something that is good for you to experience.

release of your emotions) and healthy soil (eliminate environmental toxins, hazards and things which can block its growth). Add patience, love and positivity to help your tree grow strong.

If you don't act, you may experience something people call a healing crisis. This is something that may get your attention and be incredibly demanding, such as an illness, a near-death experience or a seismic shift in your world, such as something truly shocking or unexpected. These wakeup calls manifest in different ways, but don't beat yourself up if you find yourself in one. If you're not feeling worthy of a better feeling, you may need to be shocked into attention.

On some level, though it may not look like it, this healing crisis might be a positive thing that we cannot recognize as such at first. This growth may be necessary before we can tackle another area of our lives. As Rilke said, "Perhaps everything terrible is—in its deepest being—something helpless that wants help from us."

Be patient with yourself. You didn't get to be this way overnight and healing may not happen overnight. We don't automatically wake up one day saying, "From now on, I'm going to ignore everything I've done and focus on only feeling good." It's a process, and there are things we can do to facilitate the healing.

Forgive your past and save your life

My chiropractor, Renata, recommended a CD by her teacher Dr. M.T. Morter, Jr. called **Forgive the Past and Save Your Life** (available at www.morter.com). She explained the process outlined on it, and I adapted this process into the ritual you are about to read.

FORGIVENESS: THE KEY TO THE KINGDOM

I used to think that forgiving someone for something they did in some way condoned the action, but I learned that you can separate out the individual from the act. You can forgive the soul inside of the person without ever forgiving the action that was done. The idea is to release from inside of you what you are holding onto so that you can be free to heal once and for all. It may take more than one go to achieve the desired result, but every time you practice forgiveness, you lessen the power the injustice has over you.

As Eckhart Tolle shared in *The Power of Now,* "After two ducks get into a fight, which never lasts long, they will separate and float off in opposite directions. Then each duck will flap its wings vigorously a few times, thus releasing the surplus energy that built up during the fight. After they flap their wings, they float on peacefully, as if nothing had ever happened." As humans, we need to find ways to release the energy of resentment, stress and excess emotions that build up in our system.

Crying seems like a simple way to release energy, but some of us have a hard time allowing our emotions to come out, so we many need to do something to get the process started. Some people kick-box, or punch things. Others do comedy, sing or scream at the top of their lungs. And if all else fails, we can bring in the professionals and try a variety of methods, such as emotional release work, Reiki or Bio-Energetic Synchronization Technique, which has been known to help patients deal with post-traumatic stress disorder.

Exercise: The forgiveness ritual

Forgiveness is about letting go of the resentments that are being stored in your body and weighing on your heart. Forgiveness is a way of rebalancing something that was imbalanced. It is a way of shining light into the darkness of our past and allowing us to feel more peace and freedom.

The following ritual follows a three-step process. It's about forgiving the other individual, even if you can't forgive the act that they performed. It's about forgiving yourself for anything you may have done, consciously or unconsciously, to contribute to or put yourself in the situation. Lastly, it's about giving the other person unconscious permission to forgive you for anything you may have done, consciously or unconsciously.

I like to perform this ritual near or in water (a tub, shower or waterfall.) Sit or lie back and close your eyes. Pay attention to your breathing. For each one of the following steps, you are going to hold your breath for as long as you can. Once you release the air, immediately take another deep breath and hold it for as long as you can. Repeat this a total of three times for each section below.

To sum up, you will spend:
- 3 BREATHS forgiving another
- 3 BREATHS forgiving yourself
- 3 BREATHS giving others unconscious permission to forgive you

There will be nine breaths total for one round of the forgiveness ritual. Repeat it as often as feels good to you. Many people have found this process to be incredibly healing.

STAGE ONE Inhale deeply and hold it. Picture a situation that is particularly stressful to you. Visualize the players involved. See if images come to mind, or words that may have been exchanged, or things that you wish had been said or done differently. Consider the phrase "Given our view of the world at any given time, we are always doing the best that we can."

The other people involved, given their view of the world, were also doing their best.

As Master Saint Germaine once said, "If they knew better, they would do better." Allow whatever comes to your mind to present itself. Release and breathe normally. When you are ready, move onto step two.

STAGE TWO So much of the time, we're so focused on the other person, we don't consider ourselves. Take a deep breath and consider that we are doing our best given our view of the world. Sometimes we may not like the way we allowed ourselves to get into a situation or the way we responded to something, but it's important to forgive yourself and recognize that you are doing your best, too. Keep allowing whatever comes to your mind through the three breaths. Release and breathe normally. When you are ready, move onto step three.

STAGE THREE Take your deepest breath yet. Give the other person or people involved unconscious permission to forgive you. Whether it's something you did consciously or unconsciously (you may have simply reminded them of something else in a different part of their lives which had nothing to do with you), allow them to forgive you anyway. It may not happen at this moment in time for them, it may not happen until much later in their lives (or after this life, if you believe in such things), but the idea is similar to having two hotel rooms next to one another with a connecting door. You are opening your door, and when they decide to open theirs, they will find that you have already released the issue(s). Continue allowing whatever comes to your mind through the three breaths. Release and breathe normally.

Creativity and Future

"There are no seven wonders of the world in the eyes of a child. There are seven million." — Walt Streightiff

THE SOURCE OF INSPIRATION

What inspires you? Some people are motivated by their past, but usually what inspires us is the promise of a future. This can mean children, the family we are creating, or simply the idea of a better life. When inspired, people use words like "in the flow." Some people feel as though they are the channel for something coming *through* them, as opposed to coming *from* them.

In feng shui, the children area relates both to our future and the source

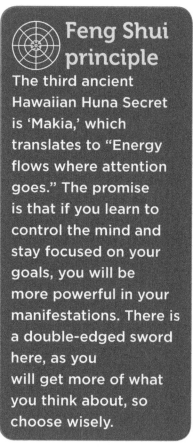

Feng Shui principle

The third ancient Hawaiian Huna Secret is 'Makia,' which translates to "Energy flows where attention goes." The promise is that if you learn to control the mind and stay focused on your goals, you will be more powerful in your manifestations. There is a double-edged sword here, as you will get more of what you think about, so choose wisely.

Color your world

The best colors for creativity and inspiration are those that represent the element metal. In feng shui, stunning white, cream and slate grey are all good support colors. Additional colors for creativity are gold, wheat, khaki and earth tones. Pure, clean, vibrant colors are best.

of our creativity. What symbolizes creativity more than the mind of a child? When we embody the characteristics of being childlike, the heavens open and we can manifest our deepest heart's desires. The degree to which we embody these principles is the degree to which we can experience magic in the world around us.

CHILDREN

GOAL: See through the eyes of a child; be open and wondrous. People that see magic in the world have a sense of innocence about them; some liken that to a child-like wonder. In the teachings of Jesus, He correlates being like a child to having access to Heaven. If any part of Heaven is here on earth, it makes sense that we would not see it by being practical, but by embracing our sense of wonder and possibility.

Many people believe that Shakespeare was one of the most creative playwrights and poets of all time. His plays stand the test of time not only because they reflect deep wisdom and use incredibly evocative language, but also because there are spiritual truths that live underneath each of the stories that are told. My friend and acting teacher, Rod Menzies, used to impress upon us that in every scene of Shakespeare you could see the qualities of *discovery* and *wonder.* To wit: "Children trust Shakespeare because they can still see the plays as play, with all the joy and wonder of discovery that this truly entails." (*Janet Field-Pickering, The Folger Shakespeare Library.*) There's something to living each moment like it's wondrous and magical, like there's possibility in the air. Children are infinitely creative in the way they figure things out and problem solve; as adults we get more limited and we sometimes lose the creative jumps that children make.

PITFALL: Little-kid logic

Our imaginations can be used to create fantastical dreams or horrible nightmares. When children start to make sense of the world, they don't have a lot of experience to draw from. Because of this, they will sometimes make jumps in logic, connecting two seemingly separate things and attempting to make sense of them in their minds. An example is the child who brings home a "C" on their report card the same week they find out their parents are getting a divorce. In their mind, it must be their fault. The child may think that if they had only done better in school, their parents would stay together. I call this type of thinking *little-kid logic.* When we take the information we have and make assumptions to fill in the blanks, that's using little-kid logic.

My mother married my stepdad when I was five years old. My first food memory is from their wedding; I can still remember their wedding cake. It was carrot, and it was the best dessert I had ever had. I went through phases with other desserts through the years, but when they divorced, I found myself ordering carrot cake at almost every opportunity. When I was asked why carrot cake, I said, "Because it is my favorite." Looking back at this, several years later, I think that there may have been a little silent protest wrapped up in my dessert eating. If I ordered enough carrot cake, perhaps my parents would get back together. I never told anyone about it at the time, but I don't think even I saw the connection. That's little-kid logic in action.

SOLUTION: Exactness, cleanliness, order

The Hawaiian word "Pono" also means exactness or in perfect order. In feng shui, when people's homes are designed predominantly with metal items and things that represent metal (whites, greys, round shapes, etc), it reflects someone who has a type-A personality when it comes to cleanliness; someone who wants everything in its proper place. Writers will sometimes clean the entire house before sitting down to write. Some people think it's just procrastination, but many of my clients have shared that they feel much more creative when their home is clean.

Cleanliness as a means to creativity

Clean house. Clean food. Clean thoughts. When our homes are in order, there is clarity of thought. When we eat clean food, our bodies are less likely to have adverse reactions that could cloud our minds. Many spiritual teachers say that when you fast, you have a clearer connection to Spirit. This is one of the main reasons why fasting is an essential spiritual and religious practice. It puts us more in touch with the invisible world that is all around us. Clean thoughts leave us feeling lighter and free from burden. When we have a clear channel, the flow of creativity can enter our hearts and our minds.

CREATIVITY

GOAL: Keep a balance between past, present and future

We already touched on the fact that our creativity is related, to some degree, on the future. In order to function in today's world, we have to plan. If we didn't, we would just float through life unproductively. It would make it harder to meet friends for a drink or to catch a movie, and we would constantly need reminders of when to show up at work. We have devices to assist with this: computers, cell phones, virtual calendars and alarms.

Despite all of this, we can't spend all of our time thinking about the future or we would miss out on everything else. We discussed in the last chapter the concept of facing our past so that it would lose its power over us. Two chapters ago, we discussed the benefits of staying in the present moment. So how do we find a balance between these three ways of looking at our life? With clients, I've created a 60-30-10 model of time management, which allows them to understand where they should be investing their time. This model also works well when considering the breakdown of past, present and future thinking. We know we want to become whole with our past so we can claim a big future and live fully in the present, but what does this look like?

Imagine you are driving a car. The road represents the present moment. The rearview mirror allows us a chance to see what is happening behind us, which could affect us in the present. The horizon (or the GPS) represents our goals or the future. If all we do is look at one of these three areas, we're in danger of never arriving at our destination. We probably spend the majority of our time staying aware of what is happening directly in front of us and around us on the road; perhaps as much as 60% of our time is spent staying present. The rest of the time, we are focused a bit further up the road. We may be looking six car-lengths ahead to see what is coming up in the near future. We may check out our GPS to see if we are advancing toward our goals. We may look at the horizon line to see if there are accidents, traffic jams or inclement weather. It's also not uncommon for us to daydream and think about some degree of our future, or to spend time allowing our minds to decompress and be creative. In all likelihood, this percentage is probably closer to 30% of our time. Have you ever driven all the way to your destination and wondered how you got there? Children constantly ask, "Are we there yet?" Both examples represent an imbalance of present and future thinking. We only need about 10% of our time to look in the rear view mirror, because life on the road is meant to inform us, but ultimately, it isn't going to help us get any closer to our goals.

As we relate this metaphor to our daily lives, we may see that a pattern is emerging, which, when applied, allows us to navigate the journey of life in a healthy way.

PITFALL: Being stuck in the past, which makes the future or the horizon a scary place.

The horizon represents the unknown. How the future looks depends on the filter we apply to viewing the unknown. It can be a scary place if we are unresolved about something from our past. If a lot of stuff is coming up for you, you may have to spend more time letting go (see the last chapter on healing the past). Until you become whole and complete, it will be harder to imagine just how big the future can get.

Overall, it's important to put the past in perspective. Doing so can serve to support our growth and evolution so we don't remain stuck. If you find yourself feeling a sense of déjà vu where something feels like it's going wrong and you're waiting for the other shoe to drop, this is a good time to remind yourself where you are—here, in this moment. It is now and it is not some other time in your past. Feeling overwhelmed by the past in the present moment may be an indication that it's time to take a break. As soon as you feel connected again, you can start back down your path.

When we come up against a wall, our first tendency is to use a tool or a solution that worked for us in the past. This can be a tricky thing, as the conditions in this moment are different than they were before. As disclaimers to financial investments always say, "Past performance is not an indication of future results." When faced with an unknown horizon and past tools no longer help, it's time to get creative. As Thomas Edison said when he was trying to find the right filament for the light bulb, "I have not failed. I've just found 10,000 ways that won't work."

Nap your way back to your creativity

I used to hate taking naps. I thought they were unnecessary, especially since I had so much energy! Perhaps being made to take a nap it was designed to give my parents a break from me, offering them some much-needed peace and quiet. Regardless, I've since gotten the lesson: naps can be magical. There is nothing that kills my creativity faster than exhaustion. When my tank is empty, there is nothing left for me to give. When I am running on fumes, I am absolutely no good to anyone. On the rare occasion that I find myself completely spent, depleted and drained by all of the commitments I have made, I know it's time to take a break: go for a walk, take a shower or switch activities. If I reach a point of exhaustion where I start to forget things, my sense of humor disappears and I feel foggy-headed. This is the best time for me to nap. Even a short retreat can replenish my reserves enough to get through the rest of the day.

SOLUTION: Tap into your creative inner genius by simply playing

Some of us are blessed with friends under the age of ten. Whether these are relatives, our own kids, or children we know through friends, I think it's important to spend some time around them, just watching. Invariably, something will be invented before your very eyes. We might be reminded of the qualities of what it was like to just play—coloring outside the lines, making a mess, inventing new rules right on the spot. It's all possible. When the world has this quality, we can once again look at things as wondrous and magical.

FUTURE

GOAL: Dream big. Allow yourself to imagine the future you wish to step into.

I often like to think about the best-case outcome before I commit to doing something. It's the only way I can stay motivated through all of the unexpected disappointments and obstacles that come up along the way. If we don't know why we are committed to doing something, it can be harder to stay motivated. One thing to consider is allowing yourself to dream big; you don't want to put a limit on your possibilities, especially before you even start on the journey. This is the time to throw caution to the wind, to break through the shackles of practicality. This is the time to envision the greatest version of the future you can see yourself stepping into. As Mark Twain said, "Twenty years from now, you will be more disappointed by the things that you didn't do than by the ones you did do. So throw off the bowlines. Sail away from the safe harbor. Catch the trade winds in your sails. Explore. Dream. Discover." At the *very least,* do this in your mind.

PITFALL: The governor

When I was younger, I wanted to see how fast my friend's car could go on the open road. During a road trip, I asked him if I could, and he agreed. We discovered that when the car hit a certain speed, it backed off and started slowing down. I tested the limit of the car several times, and each time had the same result. I noticed that the car hadn't nearly approached the limit of miles per hour on the speedometer. He explained that certain cars were equipped with something called a governor, which acts as a way to limit your top speed. It's a way of keeping us safe, lest things get out of control.

For some people, their brains work the same way. It's hard for them to wrap their brain around the possibilities of what Neal Donald Walsch (author of *Conversations with God)* calls "The Greatest Version of the Grandest Vision" of their lives. Maybe it's because they've never been asked what the greatest version of the grandest vision of their life is, and it's like trying to use a muscle for the first time. For some people, being practical is a way of keeping their expectations from getting out of hand. That's not what children do. This is something we learn through the trials and errors of life or by observing other people putting limiting beliefs on themselves.

The governor may not even be a part of our conscious mind. It can show up in many forms, including sabotage. The key is not to get depressed or angry that it's there; it is important to recognize our limits. But just like a governor on a car can be reprogrammed, we can do the same thing for ourselves.

SOLUTION: Recognize the good

The first thing is to recognize that something good is happening, instead of viewing it as something negative or something to get frustrated by. You are being invited to make space for what you say you want to call into your life—more abundance, more joy, more love, more passion. All of these things are possible when you make space for them. This process isn't always fun. You sometimes need to go into the past to excavate part of your experiences to create room for more of the good stuff. Sometimes it's like a bunch of dirt, muck and slime come to the surface. This happens so that we can release what we have been holding on to. It may have to come up to come out.

If the future is represented by the horizon, perhaps we can look to its definition for some insight. Some dictionaries say that a horizon

---

The upper limits problem

"The upper limits problem is the human tendency to put the brakes on our positive energy when we've exceeded our unconscious thermostat setting for how good we can feel, how successful we can be, and how much love we can feel. The essential move we all need to master is learning to handle more positive energy, success and love. Instead of focusing on the past, we need to increase our tolerance for things going well in our lives right now. If we don't learn how to do this, we suffer in every area of our lives. As we bump into our Upper Limit Problems, relationships suffer greatly. In fact, the greater success you achieve, the bumpier your relationship tends to be." —**Gay Hendricks** is an "imaginary line that separates earth and sky." It's like the barrier between our reality and our dreams. Even the definition indicates that the barrier is only an illusion.

A BLUEPRINT FOR SUCCESS

GOAL: Be conscious of the big picture.

As Henry Thoreau said: *"In the long run, you only hit what you aim at."* If this is true, then we want to be clear about what we are intending for our lives. Going back to the theme of win-win mentioned earlier, we always want to look for solutions that are successful in all areas, as opposed to success in one area at the expense of another area. If you find that you are manifesting success in one area of your life at the expense of another, you are creating a win-lose scenario. These tend to be unsustainable and unfulfilling over the long run. So how do you identify one of these imbalanced manifestations?

Here's an example. You are really focused on getting your career off the ground. You spend all your time thinking about your

Excellence vs. perfection

It's probably a good idea to check in on your big dreams quarterly or at least twice a year. I like the idea of setting intentions at the start of the New Year and checking in again at the summer solstice. Other people like to use their birthday or a religious new year as a time for self-reflection. There is no right way to do this, so check in as you are moved to.

I prefer to avoid setting goals or resolutions, because it can activate a need for perfection. If we don't do what we set out to do on our resolution list, it can create a sense of not being good enough, not being in integrity or always falling short of our goals. Instead, I use an intention. This feels better, because it emerges from within me and not from something outside of me. This seems to play more to a paradigm of excellence, rather than one of perfection. I can always attempt to expand into a deeper experience of life, but I can never fall short of myself.

business plan and putting things into action. You start to have some success and a thriving business. You look around and realize you aren't happy. You're looking a little pale and sickly because you haven't been able to exercise much, or put too much thought into what you are eating. And you don't have anyone to share your success with because you have been too busy to spend time with people. You have created a "win" for your business and a "lose" for your personal life. What if you aimed at having success in all areas of your life at the same time? Would you even believe it was possible?

PITFALL: The whole of anything is overwhelming

My colleague Regina Leeds has often said to me, "The whole of anything is overwhelming." This can be especially true if you look at the big picture of your life and find yourself constantly comparing where you are with where you want to go. Rome wasn't built in a day and neither are big-picture dreams. But you still need to be able to take action in order to wake up one day in the life you have always dreamed of and imagined. It won't just come and knock on your door. You have to picture it and be specific.

When you start thinking of what you want to aim at, you might find that you keep saying what you *don't* want. This can be problematic, because then you're thinking about and imagining all the things you don't want to experience. You may even have emotional responses to some of these things that can only stand to give them more power. Each time you think of something, it's like planting a seed in the ground. The emotions you feel as you picture the thing happening to you is like watering the seed. Stand back and give it time and you may wake up in a garden of weeds. But all hope is not lost.

You can use the specific things you *don't* want to help figure out what you *do* want. If you want to, you can even start a list. (Go back to the Brain Dump exercise in Chapter 1 and review it; it can be incredibly useful here.) Once you have your list, take a blank piece of paper and begin to make a list of the opposite of what you don't want. Instead of "I don't want to be poor," you might say "I'd like to be wealthy." Instead of "not alone," you might say "in a loving, committed relationship" or "surrounded by an incredible group of friends." Using what you don't want as a jumping off point can be incredibly effective for fleshing out the blueprint of your dreams.

SOLUTION: Combat overwhelm with bite-sized chunks

One of the ways that is particularly effective in creating a roadmap to a particular goal is to think backward from the end. You can lead yourself on a guided journey into the future where you come face to face with the thing you want to experience. It's almost like test driving your future and really putting yourself in the driver's seat. In this case, it's all taking place in your mind. See if you can make it as real as possible for yourself.

Start by asking a series of questions and write down what comes to mind. The first question is: What's the very last step in the process? What is it that will let you know that you have accomplished what you set out to do? For example, if you want to be a musician, perhaps your goal is to perform on stage. The very last step would be "Walk out on the stage to perform." Start by writing this down, then write the thing that comes right before the last step: "Arrive at the venue and get ready."

Even if there are holes in the exact steps, you can keep moving backward in time until you arrive at the starting point, which may be "Book the venue." Then "Promote the event." Fill in the blanks with things that make sense, even if you don't know how at this moment. This will create an outline you can fill in with bite-sized chunks. Don't overlook things; there are a lot of micro-steps. For example, if you say something general like "write the songs," it doesn't give you bite-sized chunk steps including finish the songs, sound mix them, burn onto CD, deliver final materials. Really get specific and then focus on the task in front of you.

Once you start to take the steps, you might not follow everything exactly as you imagined it. Life can be filled with happy accidents; you may meet someone who can help you bypass several of your steps. But if you can see the big picture and know what the one step is you need to focus on right now, then it's more likely you can relax. Being relaxed allows you to stay open to the flow of life. That's when magic can step in.

PITFALLS: Losing interest. Getting distracted. Not staying the course.

BONUS GOAL: **Seeing it through to completion**

It is one thing to have a goal; it's another thing entirely to see it through to completion. As Ross Perot said, "Most people give up just when they're about to achieve success. They quit on the one-yard line. They give up at the last minute of the game, one foot from a winning touchdown." The path to success may be filled with potholes and assorted dangers, but most of them are self-created.

SOLUTION: A 9-step checklist for self accountability

- ☐ 1. Want it more than you don't want it. [DESIRE]
- ☐ 2. Hold a vision of your success in your mind. [VISUALIZE]
- ☐ 3. Create a plan of action. [BLUEPRINT]
- ☐ 4. Do it every day no matter what. [DISCIPLINE]
- ☐ 5. Hold yourself accountable. [INTEGRITY]
- ☐ 6. Use your willpower to avoid distraction. [FOCUS]
- ☐ 7. Remind yourself with multiple cues. [VISUAL AIDS, ASSISTANCE]
- ☐ 8. Embrace your light and your darkness. [ACCEPTANCE]
- ☐ 9. Know that all of this is for your highest good. [TRUST]

WHEN TWO OR MORE GATHER IN THE NAME OF SOMETHING...

One year for my birthday party, I invited everyone over to make a "wish board" of something they wanted to see come to fruition by the end of that year. I had everyone bring a stack of magazines and some scissors. The intention was that when I blew out the candles, I would be helping to make everyone's wishes come true. We feasted on "foods of the gods," such as grapes, figs, tzatziki, honey, yogurt, pastries and wine. Everyone walked

EXERCISE: Create a vision board to get the future you want

A visual representation of your goals and dreams, made up of words and images that you gather from magazines, postcards, photos and other things you find.

To make a vision board, gather the following:
- A piece of foam board
- A pair of scissors
- A glue stick, rubber cement or clear tape
- Cut out words (or written words)
- Images (from photos, magazines and postcards, etc.)

As you start to assemble the board you have several options:
- You can break the board into three sections: past (left), present (center) and future (right).
- You can place something important in the center of the board and put things around it in priority of importance.
- You can use the board as a Bagua map and place the items into the nine areas of this book.

away from the evening with something unique in their hands. There was something special to sharing this experience with a group of people who supported each other's intentions.

WHERE TO PLACE YOUR VISION BOARD

After you have assembled your board, place it somewhere that you see it on a regular basis. If you don't want others to see it, put it in your room,

Pinterest

Now that pinterest.com is all the rage, you can find many of the images you're looking for online all in one place. You can create an online vision board or download images and print them out to paste on your physical vision board or book. Technology working for us!

in a cabinet or in the closet so that you can see it but others cannot. You can also make the flip side look like artwork and show that to people when they come over. When they leave, you can flip it around again.

THE VISION BOOK

Alternatives to making a vision board would be to make a book of vision pages and assemble them into a three-ring binder. You can place it somewhere special and flip through it now and then. You can also skip the vision board and make your technology into your vision board. Screensavers, passwords, the background on your PDA....each and every thing you use can be a reminder of your hopes and dreams. Use whatever works for you!

"There is a vitality, a life force, a quickening that is translated through you into action, and there is only one of you in all time, this expression is unique, and if you block it, it will never exist through any other medium; and be lost. The world will not have it. It is not your business to determine how good it is, not how it compares with other expression. It is your business to keep the channel open. You do not even have to believe in yourself or your work. Keep the channel open. No artist is pleased. There is no satisfaction whatever at any time. There is only a queer, divine dissatisfaction, a blessed unrest that keeps us marching and makes us more alive than the others."

—Martha Graham

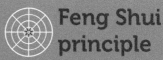

Wisdom and Self-awareness

"A human being has so many skins inside, covering the depths of the heart. We know so many things, but we don't know ourselves! Why, thirty or forty skins or hides, as thick and hard as an ox's or bear's, cover the soul. Go into your own ground and learn to know yourself there." — Meister Eckhart

INFORMATION VS. WISDOM

Confucius stated that wisdom could be learned by three methods: reflection (the noblest), imitation (the easiest) and experience (the bitterest.) Wisdom is a personal understanding that cannot be shared directly from one person to the next. We can

Feng Shui principle

The seventh ancient Hawaiian Huna Secret is 'Pono,' which translates to "Effectiveness is the measure of truth." The message is to stay positive and know that there will always be another way. We will experience magic in our lives in proportion to the degree with which we are in harmony with the truth.

Color your world

The best colors for honoring wisdom and knowledge are ones that activate intuition, communication and the bridge between your head and your heart. In feng shui, turquoise, midnight blue and greenish-gold are all good support colors. You can also bring in black, indigos and violet.

communicate information to each other and sometimes we can imagine the experience, but wisdom comes through living an idea into action.

Reflection Sometimes we learn wisdom after the fact. This is what they mean by hindsight being 20/20. We can reflect on something that happened and replay the events and experiences of a particular situation. These often lead to "aha" moments, where we gain insight and understanding of ourselves on a deeper level (something Yasuhiko calls *innerstanding*.) Sports teams do this by "breaking down" film from past games in order to learn, grow and prepare for the next time.

Imitation Copying another person is what is meant by standing on the shoulders of those who have come before us. We get the value of others' experience and this expands our own. We can avoid the pitfalls of trial and error and have a more direct path to success. A good example of this is recreating a recipe from a cookbook. If we had to figure out a dish on our own, it would take significantly more time and resources. Or we may not attempt to cook.

Experience Once we have lived through something, we can say with authority that we "know something from experience." This is the mark of wisdom and inner power. You can read about something or imagine something all you want, but until you live it and experience it, it hasn't become wisdom. In order for information to transform into wisdom, it must be experienced through the heart.

WE ARE ALL CONNECTED

There are a lot of ideas floating out there. It feels as though there is something that links us all together. Perhaps there is a metaphysical world wide web, which we can all access at any time from wherever we are. All we need to do is tune into it. Perhaps you have noticed a time when two people seem to pick up on the same idea at (or around) the same time. Maybe it doesn't matter where the ideas came from. Maybe all thoughts already exist somewhere and we are lucky enough to tap into them now and again. After all, a good idea is a good idea regardless of where it comes from.

Sometimes, conflicting ideas result in confusion. We may hear angels and devils that sit upon our shoulders, the voices of our parents warning us of danger, or the voice of our hedonistic selves wishing to be fulfilled. We may hear spirit guides, long lost souls or our relatives who have passed on. We may hear a voice based on our past experiences, or the voices of our unborn children urging us to "find our soul mate" so they can be born. Our own voice lives in the middle of it all. With all of these thoughts floating around, one has to ask: whose thoughts are you thinking?

One of my best friends in high school, Christopher, and I signed up for the same art class. Though the topics of our art projects were very tranquil (such as a drawing of a bowl of fruit), we would spend the entire art class debating at the top of our lungs. The reason we did this, we realized later (possibly in our other shared class, psychology), was that we were parroting exactly what our fathers had said to us and we were taking their

"In self-awareness there is no need for confession, for self-awareness creates the mirror in which all things are reflected without distortion. Every thought- feeling is thrown, as it were, on the screen of awareness to be observed, studied and understood; but this flow of understanding is blocked when there is condemnation or acceptance, judgment or identification. The more the screen is watched and understood—not as a duty or enforced practice, but because pain and sorrow have created the insatiable interest that brings its own discipline—the greater the intensity of awareness, and this in turn brings heightened understanding."

—Krishnamurti

words as our own truths. We were debating to figure out what we actually thought, as opposed to the voices that were running in our heads. (This story picks up again in the section *Get to know yourself*)

THE AUTHETIC SELF

There is a voice that exists deep within us that knows what is best for us more than anyone else in the world. This voice has more insight than our parents, our therapists and our psychics combined. This is the voice of our authentic self. How many times and in how many ways have we heard about this? *The kingdom of God is within you* (Luke 17:21). *All power comes from within* (Hawaiian Huna principle #6: MANA.). *To thine own self be true* (Shakespeare.) It is implied that there is tremendous wisdom, power and possibility that lies deep within us.

Yasuhiko likes to refer to the egoic self with a lower case "s" (self) and the authentic self with a capital "S" (Self). This is what is meant by "get out of your own way," "get out of your head" or "give over to a power greater than yourself." Some people would refer to this voice as an angel, a spirit guide or the voice of God. This authentic Self is available to us anytime we wish to access it, but we have to be still enough to hear it.

GET TO KNOW YOURSELF

Most of us don't spend a lot of time thinking about ourselves. We are taught that it is selfish, conceited and arrogant. The danger, we are told, is that we may become a narcissist, someone who relates everything in

Namaste

In India, people greet one another by putting their hands in prayer position and saying "Namaste" (sounds like na-ma-stay). It is a greeting that means **my highest self acknowledges and honors your highest self. We are one.** This is also a greeting you might hear at the beginning and end of a yoga class. It offers respect to not only the teacher of the class, but also the deepest part of ourselves.

the world back to me, Me, ME. If we spent every waking second thinking of only ourselves, it's true that it would become problematic, but there must be a balance between always thinking of ourselves and never thinking of ourselves.

While it isn't clear which of the ancient Greeks actually said "know thyself," it's attributed to at least six different philosophers and was supposedly written at the temple of Delphi. The message is clear: we cannot honor our deepest self without spending some time becoming more aware of this intimate part of ourselves.

An added benefit of knowing ourselves is that it allows us to communicate our needs, preferences and desires to others. When we clearly articulate our needs, preferences and desires to others, we are more likely to get what we want than if we don't. Going back to the story about my friend Christopher and me in art class: I later realized that we were getting to know ourselves for the first time. That process evolved because as I listened to the voices within, I knew that they were in direct conflict with each other. For example, what I had been told ("it won't work") came up against how I felt, which was "I have to find a way." This was about a lot of different things in my life. This was also around the time I wanted to go to school for theater and psychology. This was the first time I considered challenging what I was told when my inner feeling indicated otherwise. I wouldn't have known this before. I'm really grateful for that time where my friend and I were screaming at each other in art class.

In feng shui, the number seven relates to wisdom. It is found throughout our culture as a number that represents something ancient and powerful. There are seven days in a week and seven notes in an octave, seven colors in a rainbow, seven chakras in our energy system. In the spirit of wisdom, here are seven ways to access your true inner wisdom more deeply:

1 TAKE QUIET TIME

If we don't take the time to be quiet, our authentic Self may not be heard. Many of us who live in cities suffer from noise pollution. Listen to the world for a minute or two. What do you hear? Maybe there's a television on in the background to keep you company and music playing on the radio. There may be people screaming at each other down the hall, honking horns from the street below and a fire engine blaring down the next block. Where is the room for your authentic Self in the midst of all this noise?

Get quiet. Start out with just a few minutes and see how it goes. If it flies by and you are craving more of it, do it again. Consider it your "mental smoke break." People still go outside to take smoke breaks, so why can't you turn off the lights and take some quiet time? Or walk around the

Unplug/turn off your technology

Have you ever heard of a technology vacation? It may be the way of the future. This is where people go to a hotel or retreat center and they don't bring anything with them (or they leave them in the car.) Rather than checking your cell phone every few minutes or going onto your laptop to send "just one more email" or turning on the TV "just for a few minutes," you spend time doing other things. There's so much electromagnetic pollution in the world that going somewhere to take a break can be an amazing experience. It can also do wonders for your energy.

At first, you might find yourself distracted by consistently wondering what is happening "out there." Then, after a while, this layer may fall away. You may find that you are having so much fun that you forget all about the rest of the world. And then this layer may fall away too. You may find that you experience a peacefulness, stillness and presence that you haven't felt in years.

If it's really this great, why don't we do this all the time? We may be as much distracted by fear as we are by the things we are working toward achieving. You may say to yourself **my boss might call and be mad if she can't get me, or if I don't respond immediately via email; I have to look productive; I can't lose this job; bad things will happen!!**

Consider for a moment what would happen if you had no choice in the matter. What would other people do if you were truly sick, injured, out of the country, or dead? If you literally could not respond to people, they would adapt. Perhaps it's not best to test this theory when you are under deadline or someone is waiting for something time-sensitive. Under relatively normal circumstances, try putting this activity to the test. Start out with 3 minutes and if all goes well, move up to 15. Maybe you will find that taking 30 minutes or an hour or your full lunch break away from being connected to everyone is ok. When you come back to your technology, you might find that the world continues on and people find a way.

And in the rare instance that someone gets annoyed that under normal circumstances you couldn't get back to them within an hour, perhaps this is an invitation to a conversation that needs to take place, a new boundary that needs to be set, or even a new profession that needs to be pursued.

block and just breathe. Even if you have to buy a white noise machine to block out some of the persistent sounds or purchase some noise-cancelling headphones, a little bit of quiet may be just what the doctor ordered.

2 NAVEL GAZING

We went over different meditation techniques in the chapter on health. Meditation allows our mind to be the calm amidst the storm. One might go deeper than simply blocking out sounds and external stimulations and instead focus on their breath, a word or an image. When we meditate, we strengthen our mental muscle so we can choose what to focus on. We can learn to choose our thoughts instead of our thoughts choosing us.

Meditating doesn't guarantee that we will always be the master of our thoughts at all times. Sometimes a situation will trigger us in a way that makes us freeze, or react in a way that we later regret. Like any muscle, exercising it doesn't mean we will become superhuman, but we certainly may find that we have more options when situations arise, or that the recovery period from being triggered will be significantly reduced. Our inner guidance is available to us at all times; it's just under the surface, which is why we need to meditate and get quiet to hear it.

3 ACT ON YOUR WHISPERS OF INTUITION

Once you practice getting quiet, you may start to notice things. Hunches. "Spidey" senses. Whispers of intuition. At first you may doubt that you are hearing anything worth listening to. Sometimes the hunch may not make logical sense, but if you pay attention, it may turn into something of value. How will you know if this is your guidance if you don't listen to it? When I'm in the flow and I listen to this voice, I'm astonished by the results.

A couple of years ago, I was at a Dodgers game. I experienced a strange few minutes where I just knew something was going to happen. I stood up and announced to my three friends that the next batter was going to hit a home run and I pointed to the exact spot where he was going to hit the ball. Wouldn't you know it? The next pitch, the batter did just what I had predicted. My friends were astonished. It's not something that I felt I could control or make happen. It was just a moment where I knew something and when I acted on it, the universe backed me up. These are the things that make me believe in kismet, synchronicity and serendipity (three of my favorite words). Those are available to us at any moment.

There are times when I don't listen as well, and as a result, things don't turn out as well. It's like the story about the guy who is in the middle of a rainstorm. A truck comes and offers to bring him to safety. He stubbornly refuses and says, "No thanks, God will save me." Then a boat comes. Same response. A helicopter follows. He refuses, again saying, "God will save me." He drowns. Now he's waiting in God's office, fuming. The big guy swivels around in the desk chair and this guy lays into him. "I believed in You. I told everyone that I had faith in You. I said You would save me and You let me die. What gives?!" God sighs and says: "First I sent the truck…"

I find that life tries to get my attention in three different ways. The first stage is usually pretty subtle. It may be a recurring image, a feeling or an idea; something that gets my attention and stands out from other feelings or ideas. I can be a bit stubborn. In the past, it has taken a second time or a third time of noticing something before I felt as though the universe was really trying to get my attention.

The second stage is usually less subtle. It feels more like a tap on the shoulder. "Hey. You. Stubborn guy. Pay Attention." I may hear it this time, but may not act on it right away. I may say, "Yeah, yeah. I'll get to it."

If I don't act on the intuition in a timely fashion, the universe gets more forceful. This is the time when I may get sick and realize I need to slow down, or something may be taken from me that was getting in the way. If the universe really wants to get my attention, it will. Now that I realize this, I've made a pact with the universe that says: *I'll do my part and listen, but please be extra clear if you have a message for me* so that I can hear it the first time.

Those first stages are one aspect of the divine working for good. The second is more forceful and insistent. The third one really, really tries to get our attention. Hopefully we listen to the first one or two. But given the option to do things the easy way, the medium way or the hard way, why always choose the hard way? You may know you are hearing something but may not have any idea how it is going to work out. Sometimes listening to those inner whispers of intuition requires a tremendous leap of faith.

4 PAY ATTENTION TO YOUR DREAMS (WHISPERS OF INTUITION YOU RECEIVE WHILE ASLEEP)

The universe is pretty sneaky. Even if we are still developing our practice of hearing whispers of intuition during our waking lives (or if we flat-out refuse to acknowledge their existence—for whatever reasons), our intuition still speaks to us every night, in our dreams.

Nighttime is when we recharge. Our bodies get rid of toxins, our energy system recharges its batteries and our higher self connects to our source, however you want to view that. Some people like the image of a spiritual counsel, guardian angels or God. Some people don't believe in the idea of a God, but they may believe in their higher self. Since we are talking about something that is formless making its presence known to you, pick whatever image works best for you. Just before bed, ask that part of yourself a question. When you wake up, see if you've received a response. You might keep a dream journal beside your bed and jot down notes when you wake up and remember your dreams. In it, you can review your questions from the night before. If it only ends up being a creative exercise for you, it can still have tremendous value. If it ends up being more than that, perhaps you will begin to feel more supported by the divine than you've ever experienced before.

5 ASK YOURSELF A SERIES OF THOUGHT-PROVOKING QUESTIONS

On a less subtle level, you may find that a good way to hear what your inner voice has to say is to talk to it. It's similar to the experience of asking yourself a question before bed and waiting for your dreams to show you a response. In this case, you're looking for your inner guidance to respond. As we discussed in Chapter 3 on fame, there can be tremendous power in asking questions. Excellent examples of this are the *Conversations with God* books by Neal Donald Walsch or the *Teachings of Abraham* by Esther and Jerry Hicks.

At first you may feel odd asking yourself a question. It may feel as though someone is judging you, or you may simply feel like nothing is

Spiritual in-case-of-emergency card

When dealing with button pushers, you may feel anxious, angry or pushed over the edge. During these times, it can be really helpful to have an emergency action plan in place that you can refer to so you can regain your composure quickly.

One thing that I like to work on with my clients is a "spiritual-in-case-of-emergency-card." It's a plan for what to do when faced with an emergency, step-by-step. The goal of the card is to take any thinking out of what to do when the BLEEP hits the fan. In one section of the card you would list the phone numbers of three pre-appointed contacts who have agreed to be there for you if you are ever severely triggered by something and need to reach out to them.

When things get crazy, first, remove yourself from the situation. Go to your room, your car, or excuse yourself to the restroom if you're in public. Pull out your spiritual in case of emergency card and follow it one step at a time:

1] Breathe. Take a few deep breaths until you start to feel more calm.

2] Put it in perspective. Ask yourself some really important questions: Will this matter in a month? Will this matter in a year? Try to reframe the situation; it may not be as dire as you first thought.

3] If breathing and reframing the situation don't work, then call the people listed on your card and ask for help. These people can be alive or dead; they can be people you have actual phone numbers for, or people you call upon, like a deceased relative, guardian angel or God.

It's really important to have people that agree to be willing to pick up the phone for you should you get triggered and need someone to reach out to. If you get voice mail, since you've made an agreement that you can call them, vent into their voice mail. Hopefully that will allow them to hear it and get back to you at their earliest convenience.

If you do have the opportunity to speak with someone, ask them if you can vent about what's going on. Let them know you are not trying to figure it all out right then; you're just getting out what's weighing on you at that particular moment, so you can go back into the situation calmly.

If you're home or in your car, just journal it down, brain dump and get out everything that's weighing on you. Once you've vented, do the breathing. Ask yourself if it will matter in a year, and rejoin whatever it is (go back to the situation). Hopefully that will get you through the rest of the event or situation. If you realize you're done, then remove yourself from the situation. You don't HAVE to rejoin the party.

happening. Don't worry; whatever response you have is normal. This, like anything else, is working out a new muscle, the same way you might find that it's difficult to lift heavy weights your first few times in the gym. After committing to the process for a while, you will surely start to see results, just as you do when you consistently work out.

I've had clients say to me, "Nobody has ever asked me that before." I just think that is the coolest thing; I love thinking about something that I've never before considered. Right after college, I felt the overwhelming need to read a different type of book, to journal and contemplate what I found inside. I had spent 18 years in school and felt like it was time to learn what I thought about it all. During that time, I considered some big subjects. Why am I here? What do I want to do with my life now? What happens after we die?

That time was like a semester at school, but on my own terms. I wasn't memorizing someone else's experiences. I was contemplating and meditating on the deeper truths of life. I started going to a restaurant in the east village of NYC and sat at the community table with people I'd never met before. Sometimes I would engage in spirited conversation. Sometimes my date was a book.

I also got to speak to my mom about all of this, in that last year of her life. She wasn't giving me answers; she was asking me to seek the answers to my own questions. I think that was the mark of her being such a great teacher for me. If I hadn't had those experiences, I don't know how differently I would have handled my mom's death. As hard as it was, having had time in contemplation (and time in dialogue with her about these various subjects) helped me navigate those rough waters with just a bit of Grace.

6 SEEK OUT OTHERS WHO WILL ASK YOU THOUGHT-PROVOKING QUESTIONS

If you are struggling with being both the person doing the asking and the person doing the listening, it may behoove you to ask someone else to take on the role of the questioner. The person becomes like our training wheels; they are there to help us get the process started. The goal isn't to always have them around, but merely to have them there so that we begin to trust what we're doing.

There's a range of people to choose from: coaches, spiritual teachers, philosophers, therapists and healers. All of these people are used to asking questions that can help unlock certain aspects of your inner world. Since this is your awareness, you can't do this process wrong. Even if you have an idea of who you think would be good to speak to, you may learn that there is a difference between what you think will work for you and what ends up feeling right. Stay open to being surprised. The whole process is about discovery. It's like eating an artichoke and peeling away the leaves as you get closer to the heart.

7 FIND SOMEONE WHO IS GOOD AT PUSHING YOUR BUTTONS

Nothing makes our inner voice scream like someone who pushes our buttons. This may not be a bad thing. It may be just what we need to experience in order to hear our inner voice clearly. While there are many categories of people who excel at button pushing, here are a few examples:

169

Psychics/Intuitives I go back and forth with whether or not I believe visiting a psychic is beneficial, because I feel like the person who can tell me the most about my future is myself. That being said, I have been around my share of people who are (or claim to be) intuitive. There are a lot of them out there, so find one that works for you. I like to go to people who come recommended, and I appreciate it if I can find someone who both looks for the good and offers constructive guidance. If it doesn't feel right, then keep that in mind when listening to what they have to say. The best part about the process is that regardless of whether they tell you something you want to hear or something you hope you won't hear, you will definitely have an opinion about what you are hearing.

Confrontational people (bosses, friends, people on either end of the political spectrum) Abraham Lincoln didn't surround himself with a bunch of "yes men" who told him what a good job he was doing. He surrounded himself with people who would challenge his views and get him to either reinforce or shift his position on things. There are friends who do a good job at pushing our buttons and getting us outside of our comfort zones. Our bosses can certainly challenge us on a deep level. Watching a news program where political extremists are offering their opinions gets my inner voice riled up. Do whatever it takes to hear your inner voice more clearly.

Unexpected button pushers A few examples of unexpected button pushers are children, traffic and opinionated people in the media. Children are so authentically themselves, and very often they don't have a censor or a filter. What they say can sometimes zing us in a way that really confronts our deeply- held thoughts. As for traffic, the moment I start getting a big head about how good I am at handling life, put me on the 405 freeway in Los Angeles and have someone cut me off. My favorite lesson is coming out of yoga class and having someone on the road drive aggressively. And in the media: whether it's someone on TV that I like and respect or if I'm just flipping channels to places I normally dare not go (stations that shall remain unnamed), sometimes listening to a dissenting opinion can really crystallize what's true for me. You may be surprised where these unexpected button pushers pop up in your life, but when they do, pay attention.

Family I saved this for last, because this process can come with its own special can of worms. Families are experts at pushing buttons we thought were healed and finding buttons we didn't know we had. They say that it's easy to be the Buddha in a cave, but come back into the world and see how enlightened you are. Being around your family may not always be the most comfortable thing, but it is a quick way to get your inner voice back. We don't have to agree with them and we don't have to choose to believe them. It's like using what we don't want to figure out what we do want. We can simply use what we hear as a way of getting clearer about what we think.

EXERCISE: Take a personal retreat

Many of us have incredibly busy lives and it may be hard to find time for ourselves. Our weekends are filled with errands and catching up with friends and loved ones. Our vacations may be a chance to get away and have an adventure, but sometimes we come back from a vacation and need another vacation to relax from the trip we just returned from. The invitation here is to make time that is just for you.

WHAT TO DO ON YOUR PERSONAL RETREAT

Change your relationship to time

First thing: don't set the alarm. Let your body sleep until it wakes naturally. The more rested you are, the more clearly you will hear your inner awareness. If you find yourself getting tired in the middle of the day during your personal retreat, allow yourself to rest, drift off, just be.

Nourish yourself

Listen to what you need in each moment. Make sure you're drinking enough water. Make afternoon tea. Eat fresh, healthy and delicious foods. Exercise. Do things that help rebuild, recharge and renew yourself.

Spend time in nature

Remember the benefits of negative ions. Spend time in nature. Go for a hike. Lie in a hammock. Feel the wind blow through the trees. Swim in a body of water. If you're surrounded by life, you're more likely to feel the pulse of life within you. Also consider this a perfect opportunity to take a technology vacation, so you can minimize exposure to electromagnetic fields for a while and soak up all the negative ions you can.

Get quiet

After doing something active, spend a little time being quiet. See if anything comes to you. Write a few thoughts down in a journal. Watch a cloud go by. Be still and breathe.

COMING OFF YOUR RETREAT

When you come off of a fast, you don't eat a steak or drink a glass of scotch right away. In that same sense, see if you can be gentle as you reintegrate with the world around you. Do things that give you a sense of ease.

You may not want to bring toxins into your environment like trashy magazines or reality junk shows; stay with things that are nurturing. Use mindfulness when choosing a movie or a book to read. Consider if it is something that will make you laugh or think. When considering music, perhaps you will listen to something classical or a score from a movie.

Schedule personal retreats throughout the year

These will have more significance to you if can go on or near a special occasion. You may choose to do them four times a year as the seasons change. You may decide to do it around your birthday, while you are thinking about what you want to experience for your next year on earth. Another important time of year is the New Year, whether you follow one through your religion or you use the one on the Western calendar.

Setting a boundary for yourself

To set a boundary, we have to claim time for ourselves. Things may come up which challenge our ability to do this. Work opportunities may arise. People may protest. You may be tempted with something else you have been asked to experience. This is about priorities and boundaries. If you make it a priority for yourself to spend quiet time, set the boundary, let other people know and then go do it. People should respect it. Unless you claim that time for yourself, it's not going to happen.

Sometimes to set a boundary, we have to say no to things. It may be easy to say no to the things we don't want so we can say yes to the things we do want. It may be harder to say no to the things we want, in order to say yes to the things we **really** want. Just because something is offered doesn't mean we have to say yes right away. We can use discernment and that will pay off over time. Ultimately, setting boundaries allows us to have more freedom in other areas of our lives.

One client of mine was trying to make a decision about a relationship. There were certain things that needed to be said to create a boundary, but she was afraid to say them because she didn't want the relationship to go away. She decided to say no to the relationship, and it ended up coming back to her later (the same person) in a much better form. If it hadn't been the same person, it would have been a new person who would have met those boundaries.

Faith and Benefactors

❝Take the first step in faith. You don't have to see the whole staircase, just take the first step.❞ — Dr. Martin Luther King, Jr.

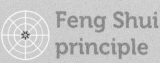

Feng Shui principle

The sixth Hawaiian Huna Secret is 'Mana,' which translates to "All power comes from within." The invitation here is to be confident and take a step into the unknown. Trust that the world will rise up under your feet. According to your faith, so it shall be.

HONORING THE INVISIBLE

The system of feng shui is designed to help people to cultivate more "chi" (good energy) into their lives. Feng shui literally means wind/water. To me, water represents everything that is visible (or can be experienced with the five senses) and wind represents everything that is unseen or invisible within a space. So how do we honor that which cannot be seen?

Some people have a hard time wrapping their brain around the concept of "energy." Depending on who you speak to, anything beyond the five senses is either very real or

Color your world

The best colors for honoring faith are those that indicate mystery, purity and spiritual awakening. In feng shui: pure whites, earthy greys and heraldic golds are all good support colors. Also good are blue-ish purples, mysterious blacks and saffron oranges.

something very "out there." Though western science is continuing to catch up to some of these ancient principles, it very possible to see the effects of energy in our everyday lives. Just as you cannot see the wind, you can very much still see the effects that wind has on the world.

But what about the times we cannot see the evidence? To embrace this concept, it requires a leap of faith into the unknown. Because there is so much emphasis on that which cannot be seen, this area is also related to our spirituality or faith. One definition of faith is belief in something for which there is no proof.

Until something shows up in our lives, we may have to read the clues left behind by invisible hands. Other people believe in "signs" or they get the feeling that people are on their side in the form of a teacher, helpful person or benefactor. Some people describe this as synchronicity, when everything just seems to work out.

It's a wonderful thing to sense that the world (or universe) has your back. What do we do when the world seems to have turned against us or when things don't seem to work out in our favor? This is an invitation to lean into people and things that reconnect us to our faith.

BE HELPFUL TO OTHERS

I've heard it said that the fastest way to get anything in life is to give it away, because you can't give away anything you don't have. What happens if you feel like people aren't being helpful or the world isn't cooperating with your hopes and dreams? Start being helpful to someone else.

Tithe If you feel moved to tithe, perhaps you can create a scholarship for someone or help someone purchase a meal. Any time you help someone toward their dreams, the world will start to help you toward yours.

Small gestures Nothing can make a person's day like an unexpected gesture of kindness. Bring your co-worker a cup of coffee. Bring the construction crew some bagels. Write thank you notes. When people feel like they are being thought of and appreciated, it can positively change the way it feels to exist in the world—for you and for them.

A "registry" for life My biological dad's spiritual teacher, Hilda Charlton, used to say, "Give the world what it wants until it wants what you have to give." This can be interpreted in different ways, but it starts with listening to what people say. When couples get married, they put together a wedding registry so that it is more likely they will get things that they really want. If you pay attention to what people say on a daily basis, you may pick up on little clues about their favorite things. I call this a "life registry," but it is basically a list of people's preferences. When you go to dinner at someone's house and you bring the host their favorite wine, they will be touched beyond measure.

Be of service If you don't feel like you can do something financial, you can always volunteer your time. Being generous hearted starts with an attitude, so even the intention to be of service might unlock limitless possibilities. Ask yourself: What can I do today? How may I be of service?

Give words of encouragement When I was first learning how to do yoga, I remember my teacher coming over with a kind word about something I was doing. I also remember how positively it affected my practice for the rest of the class. Sometimes a little bit of encouragement is all it takes to make someone's day.

Smile Smiling at someone is free and can be infectious. My mother had the ability to connect deeply with complete strangers, and I am convinced that she won them over with her smile. Sometimes a well-timed smile can get someone out of their head and back into the moment.

Lend an ear Listening to another person and allowing them to be heard can really lift a weight from their shoulders. Allow people to vent or confess something they have been holding back. When their burden is lighter, then they will be more likely to listen to others and pay it forward.

Thoughts and prayers There are studies that show that people are connected through the thoughts that they think. Just as our own thoughts can change the way our bodies function, there are studies that have shown that thoughts from other people can affect us as well. Sending thoughts and prayers is a simple, easy thing to do and can pay huge dividends in peoples' lives.

THE LAW OF KARMA

Like attracts like. Good karma creates good karma. We all have different experiences and expressions of the same principle: you get more of whatever you give.

One of the things Yasuhiko always told me was if you give to others, you'll receive twice. The first thing you receive is the good feeling that comes from your actions. The second thing you receive is the ripple effect from your actions as they come back to you (sometimes directly from the same person, but more than likely from somewhere else).

Hold the door. Let someone ahead of you in traffic. Be the bigger, more gracious person. And always follow The Golden Rule: Do for another as you would have them do for you. Certain people seem to move like this through the world and they always seem to have an infinite supply of help when they most need it. As Gandhi once said, "Be the change you wish to see in the world."

START WHERE YOU ARE

If you want more help in your life, start by recognizing what you already have. It seems to be a universal rule that as you focus on what you have, you will draw to yourself more of the same. You may be surprised to learn that you have more help than you think. This may also lead to appreciation for what you have and activate more help to make its way to you.

At first it may be difficult to recognize people who are helpful because we don't often stop to recognize them in our daily lives. You may soon discover yourself grateful for a range of people, from those who work behind the scenes to make our society function: people who grow our food, maintain our roads or keep us safe from harm (firefighters, police and military personnel.) There will soon become a list so vast, it will be hard not to feel much more connected to the people in the world around us. Soon we come to realize that very little in life gets done in a vacuum and it really does take a village of helping hands.

Consider the people around you that you consider to be helpful people or even benefactors. Here's how to define them: a helpful person can be someone who opens a door for you, or a nice customer service rep on the other end of the phone. A benefactor is someone who gives you your big break (perhaps they invest in your film or provide you another opportunity to achieve your dreams.) The common denominator between both types of people is that they lend you a hand.

The helping hand

A hand has five fingers. Would it surprise you to discover that in feng shui, the number that relates to helpful people or benefactors is five? Sometimes I take this metaphor a little further and I like to think of each of the fingers on my hand representing a helpful person. My thumb represents being there for myself. My index finger represents the spirit realm and everything unseen. My other three fingers may represent a trinity of helpful people or benefactors.

It can be a good idea to keep a list of helpful people nearby, in case you ever need to be reminded of what is most important. Refer to your spiritual in-case-of-emergency card (see pg. 167 for a reminder) whenever the need arises.

ASK FOR HELP

Sometimes in life we have to come out and ask another person for assistance. A lot of people have a hard time with this. Maybe we don't feel worthy or we are worried it will make us look weak. Perhaps we feel it opens us up to criticism that we don't want, or we want to do everything on our own. Regardless of the reasons, at a certain point you may decide you want help from another person, even if you don't know how to ask or know exactly what kind of help you need.

It can be very helpful to have clarity about what you are asking for. I remember receiving a ten-minute voicemail message from someone who once wanted a ride to the airport. There were so many apologies, hints and phrases like "If you don't want to, I totally understand," and by the time I finished listening to the message, I felt exhausted. After calling back, we ended up talking for another fifteen minutes. If they had just asked for what they needed, I could have decided how I felt about the request and given them an answer. Instead, in addition to fulfilling their request, I also had to convince them that I was okay with their request. See if you can make your requests clear and simple.

There are two realms you can ask for help from: the seen and the unseen. Although some of these ideas might seem a little strange to you, it can help if you start with what you know and work your way into what seems a little further from your understanding.

THE SEEN

Inner circle Start with the people closest to you. Ask your friends, your lovers, your teachers and your family for help. You know them well, so they are most likely the people who will help you with your request.

Outer circle Next, move to people outside of your immediate circle. These can be acquaintances, colleagues and friends of friends. They may not have as much loyalty, but they may be more than willing to assist you on your journey.

Strangers The next level consists of people you don't know. This can range from organizations to strangers you meet to celebrities (individuals in the public eye.) It may feel like a stretch, but you'll never know if you don't ask. What have you got to lose?

Beyond We don't have to ask for help only from the living. People ask for help all the time from sources that might seem a little bit out there. Sometimes people wish on a shooting star, or they believe in the influence of a planet (astrology) or they may make a request of Mother Earth. Regardless of how strange it might seem, everything has energy to it and everything is connected.

THE UNSEEN

Just outside of our comfort zone is the invisible realm. These helpers can range from those that seem human, like Christian saints or Hindu gods, to more esoteric ideas like energy fields and angels. Again, start with what you know.

Family Some people believe that when people die, they stick around for a while to watch over us. These relatives and friends may have been people who really looked out for your best interest while they were alive, or a person with whom you had a transformative moment while they were on their deathbed. Regardless of your relationship during their lifetime, the idea that these people have our backs can be tremendously comforting when meeting life's biggest challenges. It should be easy to ask them for help; just speak to them as you did when they were alive. Then get quiet and listen.

Teachers and guides Sometimes we can ask for help from people we have never met before. Whether you call out to a spiritual leader like Jesus or ask for help from a smarty-pants like Einstein to help with your exam, these are examples of reaching out to the soul of a person who is no longer in a body. Just focus on someone who feels good to you and that you trust. (note: Just like in life, there may be people in this realm who can be a little strange, so use discretion in who you call out to.)

Angelic Realm Some people really like the idea of an angel on their shoulder. Whether you see an angel as human-like, cherubic, or as a being made of light, you can ask an angel to guide you on your journey. Angels come to us through many different religions, but they also appear in many spiritual traditions as well. An angel doesn't necessarily have to have wings, but they can be some of our staunchest allies throughout our lives and beyond.

The great spirit-God Sometimes people view God as someone who has human-like qualities. Spirit has been referred to as male, female and without form. Whatever your experience of God is, this is the source of all energy and all life. It is the formless. It is the void. Speaking directly to the source can be an incredibly powerful experience. Consider for a moment that there is no wrong way to experience the divine. As we have heard many times and in many ways, the house of God has many mansions. Think of Moses atop the mountain or Noah on the ark. Picture Jesus in the desert or Buddha under the tree. What does God look like or feel like to you?

MAKE AN OFFERING

People throughout history have accomplished the most profound things when they were doing something on behalf of someone else. The Taj Mahal was a love letter from a wealthy man to his wife. People have made it through wars and horrific conditions while thinking about helping their families and their children. Sometimes an athlete who has tremendous success will point to the sky after an amazing play. They may feel that they are receiving help from the divine, but sometimes they are also making an offering to it.

One of my favorite things about yoga class is when they ask us to dedicate a pose to someone else in our lives. I seem to have more strength, more calmness and more resolve than I do when I am simply going through my motions or doing it for myself.

One of my mother's favorite songs was *Blackbird* by the Beatles.

Although she passed away many years ago, I think of her whenever I hear it. Sometimes I play it as a sort of offering to her. It makes me happy to think of her smiling and singing and dancing wherever she is. I believe that these thoughts and feelings go somewhere. I envision them reaching her wherever she is. I have no way of proving this to anyone; I just believe that it is what is happening when I play the song. To believe this requires a degree of faith.

DOUBT IS THE GATEWAY

As we discussed in our definition of faith, it's about believing in something before there is evidence of it. In that sense, it's a spiritual thing, not something in the physical world that you can measure. Some believe God is a guy with a white beard and flowing robes, some think God is not male but female, some think God is a presence, like the force in Star Wars.

There are a growing number of people who claim to be spiritual but not religious. They believe in some kind of energy or power greater than themselves, they just might not know what that energy is. Whereas religion seems to be an outside-in approach (if I fulfill something outside of myself, then I will be fulfilled inside), spirituality appears to be an inside-out approach (our sense of God emanates from within us to the world around us). I don't want to paint religion in this context as less than or greater than spirituality; ultimately, it doesn't matter. You can have faith in God, angels, in a Messiah, in a religion or faith in humanity. Both approaches have the same goal in mind: connection to something greater than ourselves.

But faith isn't something that can be taught, and it isn't something we can give to another person. It is something that is cultivated and experienced. It's a nice idea to believe that one day we will all just wake up and believe in something, but it doesn't seem to work that way. Is there something that comes before faith? A lot of people I know tend to lean into their spiritual side when they have experienced some degree of difficulty in their lives. Before I ever believed in something, I had tremendous doubts about how the world worked. I felt alone and cut off from everything around me. I don't think I have ever suffered as greatly in my life as when I thought I was absolutely alone. That being said, I don't believe that I could have ever chosen to have faith without a healthy degree of doubt and skepticism.

THE POWER OF CHOICE

Faith wouldn't exist without doubt. We don't have evidence of God, or angels or life after death. We don't have proof of a soul, or of heaven or reincarnation. So what causes doubt to turn into faith? Choice. We choose to believe that there is something more than meets the eye. As Antoine de Saint-Exupery wrote in *The Little Prince*, "It is only with the heart that one can see rightly; what is essential is invisible to the eye."

Given the option of interpreting something two possible ways (one of which feels good to you and one of which feels awful), why not choose the more beautiful one? Let's say we are making everything up. Let's say we come from dust and we return to dust. If this is true, then what is the harm in believing in something while we are still alive? If there is no chance that we will be given proof in either direction, then why not live the answer that makes you feel the best? To me this is the most beautiful choice: the one that brings relief, comfort or joy.

LEAP OF FAITH

The invitation from all of this is to let the known lead you to the unknown. Take what you know to the edge of your comfort zone and see what is just beyond. Perhaps you are still not on board with the concept of invisible helpers, angels or God. Perhaps it feels as childish as the tooth fairy or Santa and his elves. You can still take a leap of faith into *yourself.*

Some people believe in the idea of a higher self, or inner wisdom. Some people believe that we only use ten percent of our brain and that we have much more potential than we ever realize. If this is true for you, then perhaps the leap you take is trying to go beyond what you envision yourself to be and jumping off the ledge. This is one of the biggest leaps of faith you can ever make: to expand your vision of what is possible.

If a leap of faith seems too risky or overwhelming, remember the quote at the beginning of the chapter. You don't have to do the whole journey, just go one step at a time. Everything will be revealed to you in its proper time. Perhaps instead of leaping into faith, you will start with a hop. See how it feels to test the limits of what you believe in. If it feels good, take another hop. If you hop long enough, the leaps will come.

EXERCISE: The parking fairy

When I first moved to Los Angeles, I heard about the concept of the parking fairy. Since that time, I have heard of it referred to as the parking angel, parking mojo or parking karma. But in the first experience I ever had with it, it was referred to as a fairy.

The parking fairy, as you might well imagine, helps people find parking spots, which in Los Angeles, is a very valuable thing. I was told that all you had to do was see a spot in your mind where you want to park and then have faith that it will be available for you when you get there. If you said thank you in advance, that would help too. These were normal looking (and sounding) people, so I believed what they were saying, but I had to put it to the test.

Pretty soon I was finding parking spots all over town. My friends couldn't believe my luck. I told them all about the parking fairy. Some people thought I was nuts. Other people just smiled, but everyone complimented me on my ability to find parking spots.

I continued to use this technique in other cities: San Francisco, New York, Paris. There were a handful of times I didn't find parking right away and had to drive around the block. I found that during these times, I usually found out later why I didn't find parking right away. There was an accident up ahead or a road closure or another extenuating circumstance. Life was good with the parking fairy.

I truly believed this was a way for me to practice my faith. I was testing to see if it was true. It was faith in action and when it worked, it reinforced my beliefs. Don't believe me. Try it for yourself. If it works for you, pass it along to someone else.

Epilogue
How to read this book

Now that you've finished reading the book, you have many choices as to what you do with the information and ideas in these pages. You can digest them and see how they end up filtering through your system. You can start making lists, doing the exercises and putting things into action. Or you could put the book down or pass it along to someone else. I'd like to propose another option: read the book again, backward.

When we look in the mirror, our image appears backward. Have you ever played around with this? It can be a very strange experience to look at one's reflection. It can be difficult to understand movements or know which direction is which. There is a correlation between this metaphor and the book you are holding in your hands, which is a variation on the palindrome concept.

A palindrome is something that reads the same backward as it does forward. Historically speaking, the word "palindrome" has roots from the Greek words *palin,* meaning "again" and *dromos,* meaning "way" or "direction." It was reportedly coined by English writer Ben Jonson in the 17th century. The Greek phrase to describe this phenomenon means "crab inscription" or "crabs," alluding to their backward movement and an inscription that can be read backward. One definition of palindrome is "a word or phrase that means the same thing when read in either direction."

Although there may not be a literal palindrome in this book, it was intentionally written so that the meaning could be derived while reading it start to finish or finish to start. It was written about the principles of balance, and those principles are integrated into the design and overall concept. Through the prism of balance, the book *is* a palindrome; that is to say the end is actually the beginning.

WHAT DO PALINDROMES HAVE TO DO WITH FENG SHUI?

If you look in the Preface of this book, I introduced the nine areas of life according to the feng shui principles that we use to apply to your living or work space. These areas again are: Abundance & Prosperity, Passion & Romance, Fame & How you are seen in the world, Career & Service, Health & Balance, Family & Past, Creativity & Future, Wisdom & Self-Awareness, and Faith & Benefactors. But for those of you who know a bit about feng shui, you might wonder why I wrote about them in that particular order. It doesn't have to do with numerology or alphabetical order. It doesn't relate to ancient feng shui principles, and I didn't throw darts at a dartboard. The sequence is very much on purpose.

The topics are presented in order of the reasons people pick up the phone to call me, from most frequent to least. The majority of the inquiries I get are about help in the areas of both prosperity and romance, followed by career and recognition. Then health. Then family and creativity. Last, wisdom and helpful people.

I thought that this would be the best way to go through the book, in order of the most frequently asked questions and subjects. I believe that the last two chapters (self-awareness and faith) are the cornerstones of having everything you are intending for yourself and those you love. If you understand who you are, you have the faith and trust in yourself and the world around you, then everything will unfold from there as you want it to.

With this in mind, I invite you to look at yourself (and this book) in the mirror. I believe that in order for you to be your best self, you will build your foundation on the principles of wisdom and trust, also known as self-awareness and faith. When you know yourself and what you want, you can create the vision for the greatest version of the grandest vision of your life. All that remains is the faith to know that you can accomplish your dreams. With this, anything is possible. You *can* have it all.

THE END

Resources

PREFACE/INTRODUCTION

Ariel Joseph Towne, **thefengshuiguy.com**

Nate Batoon, **natebatoon.com**

CHAPTER 1

HUNA, **huna.org**

Conscious Capitalism, **consciouscapitalism.org**

CHAPTER 2

The Missing Piece by Shel Silverstein

The Missing Piece Meets the Big O by Shel Silverstein

The Seven Habits of Highly Effective People by Stephen R. Covey

Chemin Bernard, **aneisa.com/Chemin_Bernard.html**

Karen Rauch Carter, **karenrauchcarter.com**

Warner Loughlin, **warnerloughlin.com**

Dr. Pat Allen, **dr.patallen.com**

The Secret Life of Plants by Peter Tompkins and Christopher Bird

CHAPTER 3

"The Matrix," **imdb.com/title/tt01333093**

Esalen Institute, **esalen.org**

Omega Institute, **eomega.org**

Canyon Ranch, **canyonranch.com**

The Artist's Way by Julia Cameron

The Diamond Cutter by Geshe Michael Roach

Byron Katie, **thework.com**

The Four Agreements by Don Miguel Ruiz

The Art of Happiness: A Handbook for Living by His Holiness the Dalai Lama and Howard C. Cutler, M.D.

CHAPTER 4

Julie Zipper, **juliezipper.com**

The Bhagavad Gita, Translated for the Modern Reader by Eknath Easwaran

Yasuhiko Kimura, **yasuhikokimura.com**

Wayne Dyer, **Excuses Begone, waynedyer.com**

CHAPTER 5

Morter Health System (a complete system of healthcare based on Bio Energetic Synchronization Technique), **morter.com/six.php**

Sharyn Wynters, **wyntersway.com**

Erewhon Market, **erewhonmarket.com**

The Body Ecology Diet: Recovering Your Health and Rebuilding Your Immunity by Donna Gates with Linda Schatz

"An Ancient Cure for Modern Life," by Alison Rose Levy, **yogajournal.com/health/647**

Dr. Renata Mihalic, D.C. and Dr. Ken Haboush, D.C., Purple Aura Healing Arts, **purpleaura.com**

CHAPTER 6

Eat Pray Love by Elizabeth Gilbert

Healing Back Pain: The Mind-Body Connection by John E. Sarno, M.D.

BodyTalk: a consciousness based, non-diagnostic therapy to

help heal the body; **bodytalksystem.com**

The Power of Now: A Guide to Spiritual Enlightenment by Eckhart Tolle

CD: Forgive the Past and Save Your Life, **morter.com**

CHAPTER 7

Conversations With God: An Uncommon Dialogue by Neal Donald Walsch

Regina Leeds, The Zen Organizer, **reginaleeds.com**

Pinterest, **pinterest.com**

CHAPTER 8

The Law of Attraction: The Basics of the Teachings of Abraham, **abraham-hickslawofattraction.com/lawofattractionstore/product/LOA.html**

Neal Donald Walsch, Your Life Is Your Prayer, **neadonaldwalsch.com**

CHAPTER 9

Hilda Charlton, **hildacharlton.com**

About the Author

Ariel Joseph Towne is The Feng Shui Guy. Known as "an alchemist of possibility," Ariel takes stagnant spaces in clients' homes and minds and transforms them into positive, intentional spaces where people's grandest visions of their lives are encouraged to unfold. He makes a room come alive, filling it with beauty and energy.

A feng shui expert and life coach with an international client list, Ariel loves to take ancient principles and make them simple, relatable and playful. Ariel has helped people from all walks of life: from small business owners to large corporations, single mothers to growing families and struggling artists to A-list celebrities.

Ariel has contributed content to several books including: Sadie Nardini's *The Road Trip Guide To Your Soul* (Wiley & Sons), Jessica Denay's *The Hot Mom-To-Be Handbook* (HarperCollins), Eva Christina's *Beyond The Missionary* (Penguin) and Regina Leeds' newest book in the New York Times bestselling series *One Year to an Organized Life* (Da Capo.)

Ariel has been featured in *In-Touch Weekly, YogiTimes, Natural Health,* and *Mom360* magazines. Online, he has been featured on MSN, AOL, People, Vital Juice Daily and Yoga Journal. Ariel was also a regular contributor to The Hot Mom's Club website.

For two years, Ariel had a show on Sirius satellite radio 114 called "Everyday Feng Shui," which generated some of the highest listener feedback and response for Lime Media (now owned by Gaiam) of any of their shows.

In 2010, Ariel sold a TV show called *Force of Nature* to the SyFy network. He has also appeared on the shows *A View From the Bay* (ABC), *Million Dollar Listing* (Bravo) and *Platinum Babies* (WE). Most recently he appeared on two episodes of *Rock Your Yoga* with Sadie Nardini (VeriaTV) which will be airing in the summer of 2012.

Ariel lives in Los Angeles with his wife in their fully shwayed-out apartment. They have a lovely view of the Hollywood sign. Ariel is also very tall and loves guacamole.

CPSIA information can be obtained at www.ICGtesting.com
Printed in the USA
LVOW021541080313

323416LV00012BA/13/P